D1251812

The Stratton Story

The Stratton Story

By Martha Sonnenfeld
and
Frank V. Snyder

Designer
Jeff Dickson

Photography
By Hubert Schriebl

Published by:
The Stratton Corporation

ISBN 0-9607712-0-4
Library of Congress Catalog Card Number: 81-85720

PRINTED IN THE UNITED STATES OF AMERICA
First Edition

To all those who, yesterday and today, had the vision
to know what Stratton could and would become
—and the spirit to join in the creation
of a Stratton community.

Acknowledgments

A great many people have helped enormously in this effort to commemorate the twentieth anniversary of Stratton Corporation with the writing and publishing of this book called *The Stratton Story*. Starting with some of the old history of the area, the story leads into the very beginnings of this ambitious venture and covers events and personalities of its twenty year existence. So a special thanks goes to each and every one who gave me their precious time and information for this story. If I have omitted some names and events, it was unintentional. When deadlines become a reality, and space runs out, the only alternative is to curtail the writing and conclude the book.

I want to give a very special thanks to Frank Snyder, without his help and support this book would never have materialized. And most sincere words of gratitude to Jeff Dickson whose skill and knowledge I leaned on heavily; also to Hubert Schriebl whose photographs enhance immeasurably the pages of this book. To Paul Fersen, who eased my load by assisting with interviews and profiles; to Irene and Benny Benson whose memories were among the best; and to my neighbors up the hill, Ed and Elinor Janeway, who had great faith in my efforts to pull the project all together. Finally, to private citizen, Charley Sonnenfeld, who patiently bore with me, lending his advice through pages of manuscripts and miles of galleys.

Martha Sonnenfeld

Introduction

When Tink Smith and Frank Snyder came to see me in 1960 to tell me what they were doing on Stratton Mountain, all the rumors I had heard for several months fell in place. Their particular question was what might be the reaction of the legislature toward the financing of an access road. This had been provided for Stowe, Sugarbush and Killington though these went in either over or into state-owned lands. I had been serving in the Vermont House for several terms and had just been elected to the Senate from Windham County.

I took them up to see the then Governor Stafford (now U. S. Senator) who himself an avid skier, was intrigued with the plans for the Stratton area and indicated his support for the project. Governor Keyser, who followed, also supported the request though it did not materialize until a year later. Little did I realize then the turmoil and reaction this road problem would entail.

I had known Frank Snyder from my previous Long Island days and, of course, knew Tink Smith in town as a neighbor, fellow citizen and a doer. He had guided me unerringly through the personalities and pitfalls of local and state politics. The combination of these two from distant backgrounds was a remarkable one and constituted the driving force so needed in the development that was unfolding.

The Stratton Mountain Story is the mix comprising the product of many hands and the contribution of many skills. Yet in reality it is the creation of one person through whose untiring efforts wrote much of it, whipped the rest of us to start our recollecting or write our pieces, sorted out the vast array of photographs by Hubert Schriebl and others and literally, with much help from the company records, Frank Snyder and Jeff Dickson, put the volume together. Martha Kearley Sonnenfeld is a granddaughter of an 1840's resident of Stratton, was brought up in Townshend, a proprietor of an oil business there, now married to the former owner of Stratton Mountain's first ski shop. Who could be better qualified to tell the story, both past and present, that is presented herewith? As a spectator and participant in the development that she describes I believe, even though you look mostly at the pictures, the Stratton Mountain story will delight you.

Senator Edward Janeway
South Londonderry, Vermont

Table of Contents

SECTION I

SECTION II

SECTION III

Stratton Yesterday: A Distant Past

Chapter I will make no claim to historical importance. It will reassemble a few of the facts established by town records and recorded history and lean a little on legend. In order to tell the Stratton Mountain Story of today and create a story of continuity, some of its early infancy should be re-told. Without this background, however abbreviated, this project would lack depth and foundation.

With a few exceptions, the history of Stratton is not materially different from that of other Vermont towns, but notably this town had a magnificent mountain with a distinctive and rugged terrain, and a deserved reputation for dreadful winter weather.

As a child I was fascinated with the stories told by my grandmother, who was born on Stratton in 1846, and her description of the thick, deep forest with its vast quiet and loneliness convinced me that Stratton Mountain was a place of great mystery. As far as I was concerned, that shadowed wilderness held many dark secrets, and the often told stories of hunters who disappeared in those woods and were lost forever, was positive proof that the mountain could cast a spell. I am sure there were many old-timers who felt the same way.

Although my grandmother admitted to enjoying the summers, she certainly hated the winters, which she described as "wicked." Her most often made comment was, "it snows every day on Stratton." Very likely this was so, as the seasons seemed to be more rigorous in those years. Anyway, she lived there until her marriage to a "man from Townshend," and it was quietly suspected, among the members of the family, that she was delighted to have had the opportunity to marry someone who didn't live on Stratton Mountain!

Living was truly a question of survival, not only of the weather and its hardships, but of the isolation from help and neighbors that heavy snows and extreme cold can bring. Those long, bitter winters must have been almost unbearable. Looking back, you marvel at those families who hung on to their land with such a fierce purpose. Not only hoping to improve their own pitiful lot, but also hoping to improve their little community so that it would grow and prosper. Now, nearly two hundred years later, there isn't much left to show for their struggles. For one reason or another most of them gave up their land, leaving it to be reclaimed by the woods—this so clearly told by the abandoned cellar holes, and here and there a few old family cemeteries.

The Stratton of my ancestors is gone forever, and for that I must be forgiven for having some small feelings of nostalgia, even as I know that time must change all things.

Today there is a new Stratton. The mountain and the surroundings are accommodating themselves to the business of skiing. There is a whole new culture and life built around those cold and snowy winters—so hated and dreaded by the pioneers of Stratton. Summer recreation is very much a part of this picture, an important by-product of the major business of skiing.

As always, there has been skepticism among the native Vermonters about anything new and different, and many were upset over the changes that were taking place. I recall a neighbor's comment of many years ago, "This skiing won't last; someday the trees will all grow back on those ski slopes!" I must admit I was annoyed at him for thinking such thoughts, and mentally made a note of his stupidity. Now, years later, I have learned to be more cautious in my judgment of the opinions of others; hopefully, the above mentioned Vermonter (long since departed) will never be able to rise up from his grave and say, "I told you so!"

Whatever or however one feels about this facet of Vermont's recreation industry, it certainly has become an important part of our lives today. The story of Stratton and Stratton Mountain deserves to be documented, and as far as most Vermonters are concerned, the arrival of ski business was "the best thing that ever happened to Stratton Mountain."

Early History

History tells us that Vermont was discovered in 1609, but that it remained undisturbed for generations. When Samuel de Champlain discovered the lake, which now bears his name, he also discovered Vermont. Apparently the discovery of another large expanse of land (so much land had already been discovered in this new world) didn't seem very important to him, and outside of some notes of observation, Champlain seemed to almost dismiss the discovery. Perhaps for this reason Vermont continued to remain a lonely and empty land. Incredibly beautiful, but much of it too wild and rugged for even the Indians.

Stratton Mountain typified that forbidding wilderness—the wilderness that almost discouraged settlement. Although Indians did live in parts of Vermont, there are no signs or records of Indians living in the region of Stratton Mountain. There is reason to believe that they did considerable hunting here, and particularly bear hunting. According to legend Indians called the mountain "Manicknung"—home of the bear, but for whatever reasons, this name was never adopted by the white man.

One of the questions most often asked is how did Stratton get its name? Many Vermont writers have researched this matter but have been unable to come up with a positive answer. The most likely possibility is that Governor Benning Wentworth, of the Province of New Hampshire, was responsible for the name of Stratton. This involves some explanation, and relates to the fact that Governor Wentworth went rather far afield in claiming land for his Royal Majesty, King George III. Wentworth often named the land and towns he claimed in honor of someone or something to gain favor. In the case of Stratton he possibly decided to honor the new king by taking the name from Stratton, in Cornwall, England, where the Royalists defeated the Parliamentarians in 1643. So what is definitely known is that Stratton was the name designated for this area, by Wentworth, long before settlement commenced, thus rul-

The Salmon Hole Massacre

Although this is primarily a book about Stratton, there were events that happened in neighboring villages that were colorful and truly a part of the local history. One such event took place near a settlement that would later become the village of Jamaica; and in the area that is now the Jamaica State Park.

It happened in the colonial period, before Vermont had been divided up into Grants, when there was a constant series of wars between the English and the French for the domination of the Champlain Valley. One of these wars was called "King George's War," and it took place between the years of 1744 and 1748.

At this period of time, the land extending all around Stratton Mountain and including Jamaica was unbroken wilderness, with forests so dense that traveling through them was almost an impossibility. But there were trails, not made by the white man, but by the padding moccasins of Indians who had learned from hundreds of years of traveling back and forth across this territory what were the fastest and easiest routes. They followed the river banks and lake shores, and where a trail went away from the waterway there were signs, like bent over saplings tied to the ground, pointing the course. These well worn trails were called "Indian Traces" and were now being used not only by the Indians but by the white men. One of these traces followed Otter Creek to its end, then from the eastern side of Bromley Mountain where it picked up the West River en route to the Connecticut River. It was at a pool, known as the "Salmon Hole," on the West River near the settlement of Jamaica, that an incident of great local interest took place.

King George's War was another ordeal of violence and terror for the settlers living on this new frontier. The Indians involved with the French were the Abnaki Tribe of the Algonquin Nation, and were Vermont's best known Indians—they were also Vermont's chief foes in this war, and also in the French and Indian War that followed. Indians were hired as mercenaries to kill and capture Vermonters by the French leaders, something the Indians

ing out the common theory that the town was settled by people named Stratton.

His Excellency and "The Grants"

It is more or less assumed, when speaking of Vermont history and "The Grants" that everyone understands what it all means. This is generally not so, but to tell the full history about this complicated matter would not serve the purpose of this chronicle about Stratton. But in view of the fact that Stratton was one of the towns chartered by Governor Wentworth of New Hampshire—the consequences of his notorious land deals deserves retelling in as simplified a version as possible.

Frederic F. VanDeWater in his book, *The Reluctant Republic* has written a great deal about this subject and in his sophisticated style began his chapter on Wentworth with this opening paragraph:

> "His Excellency Benning Wentworth was a graduate of Harvard College, a merchant of acumen and wealth, royal governor of the province of New Hampshire from 1741 to 1766, and the grandfather of Vermont, since he created the complex brawl from which a small nation at last was born. No man ever was a less wishful forebear. All the while he actually was grandsiring a state, he believed he was doing only a smart job of promoting."

It is important to remember that in those years the boundaries of the various provinces were not very well defined. The Province of New York owned a great deal of land as far east as the Connecticut River, and the Province of New Hampshire owned most of the land on the eastern side of that river. And it was that vast amount of land, owned by New York, just across the river from New Hampshire, and which New York seemed to ignore, that was the eventual cause of all the disputed land grants.

That New York land was just too much temptation to an enterprising man like Wentworth. Relaxing in his stately mansion in Portsmouth, this elegant Governor with the acute mind of a shrewd businessman, meditated on the limitless possibilities of land development—Wentworth style.

In 1750 he put into operation the wholesale real estate business he had been planning for quite some time. If there was any doubt in his mind about the

---

seemed to do with great zeal. Whether or not it was in their nature, it was certainly further developed under French leadership.

In May of 1748, Captain Eleazer Melvin of the colonial militia, had taken a force of eighteen men from Fort Dummer (Brattleboro) to join the British who were fighting the French and Indians along the west side of Lake Champlain. When Captain Melvin reached the battle site he found no British, instead he saw hundreds of Indians. Under the impression that they had not been seen, Melvin gave orders for a hasty retreat; to remain there would certainly result in death for both him and his men. The retreat followed the same route that led back down to the West River, and when Melvin and his men reached the Salmon Hole in Jamaica they decided to throw down their packs, shoot some salmon for a noon meal and have a rest they felt was well deserved.

It proved to be a foolish and costly mistake. Led by three Frenchmen, a large group of Indians had been following their retreat, and by taking a short cut were able to set up an ambush. Immediately the Indians attacked. Needless to say, the soldiers stopped shooting the salmon and fled, leaving behind the five who were killed in that first volley. One man, John Petty, was severely wounded and his comrades attempted to help him, but after a short distance he was left on a "pallet of pine to live if he could." One record says that his body was recovered and buried; another, that it never was found.

Frederick VanDeWater, author of *The Reluctant Republic,* briefly describes Captain Melvin's flight from the massacre, adding a touch of irony:

> "In the van of the fugitives Captain Melvin ran earnestly yet right awkwardly. A tomahawk blow had severed his belt so that he had to hold up his breaches while he galloped. Even thus handicapped, he reached the Fort, thirty-odd miles away, ahead of all his men but one!"

A copy of Captain Melvin's report to his commanding officer about this incident at Salmon Hole is in the Windham County Historical Society of Newfane. It is a full and lengthy report, and a most interesting document. The tale of the severed belt and dangling breeches are included in this report—so maybe it really did happen.

legality of this project, he justified it by pointing out the fuzzy boundaries and the conflicting claims in the charters of several New England provinces.

The plans were well ordered. Dickering with individual settlers was not Wentworth's style. With the help of his surveyors he mapped out whole townships and sold them outright. Towns not yet settled. His salesman sold these unsettled towns to groups of buyers called "Proprietors." The Charter for each township directed that the land be divided into as many lots as there were proprietors, plus six extra lots. (Two of these extra lots, and not the worst of them, were reserved for Wentworth himself.)

Essentially the proprietors became speculators of land in the towns they had purchased. Some never laid eyes on the land, instead they promoted and sold their shares to poor unsuspecting, grubby settlers who did not realize until it was too late that the land had been purchased illegally.

The New Hampshire Grants became a booming business, and one hundred and thirty-eight towns were eventually established by Wentworth. All of them on disputed land.

In the meantime, the Province of New York did nothing. Wentworth's encroachments seemed to go unnoticed and the profitable business continued unhampered.

When New York finally roused itself in indignation, years later, it was almost too late to do anything. The people who had bought their land from New Hampshire were not willing to pay New York all over again for the same land. Trouble started brewing, and that long and famous skirmish between the hated "Yorkers" and the Green Mountain Boys was the result.

His Excellency Benning Wentworth must have had a premonition of what troubles were now forthcoming, and he retired of his own volition in 1766. An old, wealthy man, owning self-bestowed land grants amounting to 65,000 acres. Surprisingly, respected and well liked in his own province of New Hampshire.

The Chartering of the Town

The following was written by Abby Maria Hemenway about the Town of Stratton in her *Vermont Historical Gazetteer.* Miss Hemenway, who died in 1890, spent her life compiling five monumental volumes of Vermont History.

> "Some fourteen years before the opening of the war of the Revolution, some of the citizens of Worcestor County, Massachusetts, had their attention called to the high lands upon the eastern slopes of the Green Mountains, now known as Stratton, and to their excited imagination they became a veritable Eldorado, and July 1761, a charter for the township was secured from Wentworth."
>
> "An exploring party was sent out and steps were taken to colonize the township, but these preliminary measures were not entirely successful. No permanent settlement was effected until after the close of the war."

Reading between the lines, and knowing what we know now of the history of those years, we can see the fine hand of Governor Wentworth directing the operations of his real estate organization. Without a doubt, some of Wentworth's jobbers had descended on the County of Worcestor, hawking titles to the virgin land of The Grants, and calling attention to the lands "upon the eastern slopes of the Green Mountains."

It is also safe to assume that the land was purchased sight-unseen, and one can imagine the reactions (and to some it must have been dismay) of the exploring party when they discovered how unbelievably wild was the terrain of their recently acquired grants.

"No permanent settlement was effected until after the close of the war." Miss Hemenway's explanation is concise and sufficient, but an understatement of the stormy years that prevented settlement of not only Stratton, but other small towns in Vermont. There were years of out and out fighting with New York over the disputed titles of land purchased from New Hampshire. Then there was the American Revolution that Vermont loyally supported, although it was not yet a part of the Continental United States. All this in addition to the problems of maintaining its own shaky independence as a new sovereign Republic.

It is not difficult to understand why twenty-seven years elapsed from the receiving of its Charter to the eventual organization of the Town of Stratton. But it did happen:

> "In 1787 the citizens of this thriving burgh determined to perfect their organization as a town. On May 31, 1788, Timothy Morsman, Solomon Gale, and Benjamin Hobbs were elected selectmen."
>
> Abby Marie Hemenway
> *Vermont Historical Gazetteer*

At this point in time, it is hard to picture the Town of Stratton as a "thriving burgh" when in 1791 the records show the population to be "ninety-seven souls." But the year 1791 was a most significant year for the Republic of Vermont—this was the year when it became the fourteenth state of the Continental United States. Something the people had wanted and had been denied for a long time. Now a steady stream of immigrants found their way to towns like Stratton. Post roads and stage roads were established, such as the one over the mountain from Arlington that went through the center of the hamlet, encouraging settlement on the land of small taxes.

The Town of Stratton did flourish for quite a number of years, but in the late 1800's it began to feel the results of Vermont's "Great Exodus" of its inhabitants to other parts of the country. It was the beginning of the end. A little town that would never be the same again.

The following are some statistics on Stratton in the year 1860:

- 366 People
- 162 Polls
- 11 Dogs
- 7 District Schools
- 4 Saw Mills
- 1 Inn (The Kelly Stand located on the stage road from Arlington)
- 1 Shingle Mill and Chair Stock Factory
- 1 Congregational Church
- 1 Tavern (where the Town Hall now stands)
- 1 Blacksmith Shop

1860 Census, courtesy of Andrew King, Town Clerk, Stratton, Vermont

A Gathering of Whigs

Daniel Webster on Stratton Mountain: Sketch, courtesy of National Life Insurance Co., Montpelier, Vt.

This early history of Stratton would be sadly lacking if mention wasn't made of this unique political rally held on a remote mountaintop in Vermont.

It was the year 1840, an election year. The Democrats, being the political party in charge of government at that time, were most unpopular. The Democrats were blamed for the hard times, banks failing, scarce money, and not enough work for the poor people.

Martin Van Buren was the president of the United States, and the opposition, the Whigs, were afraid that he would be re-elected and all the troubles would continue, and the country completely ruined!

The candidates of the Whig party were General William Harrison for President and John Tyler for Vice-President. "Tippicanoe and Tyler Too" was the campaign slogan, because General Harrison had won a noted battle at Tippicanoe River in Indiana some years before.

Daniel Webster, the Senator from Massachusetts, and the most powerful man in the Senate, had agreed to speak in Vermont at the Whig Convention. His name alone would guarantee a large turnout, but no one realized how great the attendance would be to hear this popular statesman.

To give the people on both sides of the mountain a chance to attend the meeting, a large clearing on Stratton Mountain was chosen as the location. It was close to a well known stage road connecting both sides of the mountain, which surely must have played a part in the choice of location. Needless to say, the people of Stratton were enthusiastic and much preparation went into this event. The site was a 300-acre clearing, the building a big, brand new log cabin 100 feet long and 50 feet wide. The log cabin was also the theme of the convention, because Harrison was supposed to have lived most of his life in one.

Nearly every town for fifty miles built a replica of a log cabin, hitched horses or oxen to it and accompanied by the official delegation from their respective towns, made the long, hard trip to the mountain site to demonstrate and parade in front of the speakers platform. There was singing, shouting and lots of socializing. According to many reports, a considerable amount of hard cider was consumed.

It should be pointed out that to have a political rally in Vermont to prevent the re-election of President Van Buren of New York was almost unnecessary. Vermont still hated the "Yorkers" in 1840 as much as it had during the war over The Grants. But it was a great excuse for a party—and a big one!

Seriously, what made that convention such an extraordinary and successful affair was the presence of Daniel Webster, that compelling man with the great intellect and the ability to speak with overpowering conviction. No one is sure of the exact attendance because records differ, but whether it was 15,000 or 20,000, the fact remains that thousands made their way over uneven roads, traveling great distances and camping in the wilderness in order to hear the great Webster speak.

There is a monument commemorating that speech not far off that road leading down into Arlington from Stratton village. The road is not an important road any more; the clearing is over-grown and the log cabin long gone. But that political moment in Stratton's history will never be forgotten.

Winhall

Winhall, as the sister township of Stratton, has always played an important part in the history of Stratton Mountain mainly due to the fact that the Mountain is partially within its borders. Without Winhall there might not be a "Stratton Story," so it is important to include some of its earliest beginnings which might add a little more depth and feeling to the history.

In the same year that the township of Stratton was chartered, so was the township of Winhall. It must have been a busy year for the Governor of New Hampshire as he granted charters to more than sixty towns in just that one year—all of them would be called New Hampshire Grants.

Although the charter was granted on September 15, 1761, "To one Osee Webster and sixty-one other proprietors" it took several years for these proprietors to establish a market for their shares, also called lots or rights. Very few of the proprietors had any intention of moving to this new frontier; the majority were plain and simple land gamblers. This was true in a great many of the newly granted towns. Incidently, calling these surveyed tracts of land "towns" was a bit of an exaggeration as they still consisted of only virgin forest and almost totally uninhabited land.

Even though prices of shares in certain townships were going up to ridiculous extremes, disheartening reports depressed the shares in other areas. Winhall appears to have been one of those areas. Tales were being circulated by some returning settlers of the difficulties in locating their inaccessible lots. This, coupled with the beginning rumors that trouble was brewing with the Province of New York over Wentworth's grants, slowed down the speculation in Winhall real estate.

There is some evidence that eventually there were some proprietors so discouraged with their land shares that they gave them up entirely, completely relinquishing all claim. According to Zadock Thompson's *History of Vermont:* "In 1772, to induce people to settle in Winhall, many were given land." (By what authority this was allowed is not known.)

If there was panic among the original buyers of New Hampshire Grants it started with the Royal Edict of 1764, which reestablished firmly and finally, that the Connecticut River was indeed the boundary line between New York and New Hampshire.

If Governor Wentworth was trouble for Vermonters, then Cadwalder Colden, Lieutenant Governor of New York was more trouble. By all reports, Colden was a cantankerous old man, who at intervals ran the colony with an iron hand when no Royal Governor was in charge. As soon as the official announcement came affirming the old boundary lines, Colden planned a course of action. Not only did he impose expensive New York fees on holders of New Hampshire Grants but he started issuing land grants of his own, causing much anger and confusion. There have been reports that a number of Colden's New York Grants showed up in Winhall, overlapping lots already granted by New Hampshire. It all added up to a small war and reasons for delay in settlement.

In 1778 Winhall was still a wild and unbroken country, and the following account from Hemenway's *History* tells about a Mrs. John Brooks, who came from Montague, Massachusetts: "It was then a wilderness from the middle of Jamaica to Winhall (nine miles). I rode on horseback through this wilderness, guided only by marked trees; and carried a child in my lap. We lived in a small log cabin that summer, and I did not see a woman for six months. We returned to Montague to remain through the first winter. We raised plenty of apples from seed in fourteen years." (It is interesting to note that a John Slade, who is a native and life-long resident of Winhall, is a direct descendant of this Mrs. Brooks.)

The first settlement was called Middletown, and it had a common around which the first houses were built. The location was in the area where today the Winhall Hollow Road crosses over to connect with Route 30. There are no signs left to indicate a village ever existed, nor does there appear to be any information about how long it was in existence. There is a Middletown cemetery with gravestones that have many of the names of those earliest settlers, proof that the beginning of Winhall existed nearby. Bondville became an organized village in 1796, and John Slade tells this story about the naming of the village but he emphasized that it probably was more story than fact—it had been told to him years ago by an elderly aunt:

> "There were two gentlemen, prominent figures in the yet unnamed community, and each gentleman was most anxious to have the village named after him. Their names were Mr. Bond and Mr. Hubbard. After many discussions, much argument, and finally a real honest-to-goodness fist fight, Mr. Bond was declared the winner and the village became Bondville. To show his appre-

ciation of this great honor Mr. Bond deeded his house to the Methodist Church for a much needed parsonage."

Incidentally, the first settler of Bondville was a Silas Hubbard. It is an interesting speculation that he might have been the defeated "Mr. Hubbard."

In spite of a slow beginning, Bondville became a flourishing community, outdoing her sister town of Stratton, and surviving better than many others, the problems of the times.

Some statistics for the year 1860

Population:	741 Souls
Churches:	Two—Methodist and Union Congregational
Post Offices:	Two—Bondville and Winhall
Schools:	Eight—the only one remaining today is the "Grahamville School" which is now the town library.

There were also nine sawmills, one gristmill, and a chair factory owned by A. P. Graham. This factory was located in the area of the present fire station and it did a large volume of business. Interestingly, the rocking chairs made by A. P. Graham in 1860 are much sought after by today's antique dealers. There was one "extensive tannery" owned by a John and William Cudworth; and lumbering was becoming an important part of the economy. "The sawyers have constructed a slide which conveys the lumber from the steam mills on the summit of Stratton down its west side to Manchester." (Hemenway's *History*)

Today, the village of Bondville has become the front door to the Stratton Mountain resort area. This has put an increasing amount of pressure and responsibility on this community, but the people have taken it in their stride. As one resident said, "When we allowed the access road to begin right in the middle of our village, I think we did our part in putting Stratton Mountain on the map."

A Little Town Finds Faith

As you drive up the Stratton access road and approach the base area, there on your left is the Chapel of the Snows. It is a beautiful little chapel. It looks solid and dignified, as though it would last forever. Hopefully it will last a long time, and generations of skiers and their families will continue to use this lovely and unique house of worship. But it should be remembered there is another church, on the other side of the mountain in the old town of Stratton—not that far away. Once upon a time it too was beautiful in its simple and austere New England design. It was a visible expression of the solidity of the community and the people were proud of that small accomplishment. Today that church is unused and almost forgotten, along with the story of how it all happened and the reasons why.

It is not likely that the first white man to settle in the deep woods of Stratton was at all concerned about his religion. The grueling task of merely keeping alive was more immediate than his salvation. In addition, the project of hacking out a clearing and cutting enough logs for the walls of a cabin was a dawn-to-dusk job, leaving little time for religious contemplation. But in 1750, when more and more land had surrendered to the back-breaking hard work of those few early pioneers, there was one person over in New Hampshire who was busy including religion in his master plan for the settlement of the areas that someday would become the state of Vermont. That person was his Excellency, Governor Wentworth of the Province of New Hampshire—a controversial and fascinating character, who made a considerable impact on the local history. However, his influence peddling with the powerful Anglican Church by including special provisions in the town charters, is another side to this story that is not known by many.

Wentworth and His Glebes

When his Excellency drew up his plans for the royal grants, he carefully directed that each township set aside extra lots; including one for the use of the Church of England and one for the use of the Society for the Propagation of the Gospel in Foreign Parts—called the Gospel Society for short. These lots were (and still are) called glebe or lease land, and originally each one contained 250 acres more or less. Any income from these lots belonged to the Church.

Wentworth's reasoning was probably not one of philanthropic persuasion, rather it was a calculated gesture to insure support from the right people in the event that there were any problems with his questionable land deals.

There were many years and many changes in the

country before Stratton was to become an organized town, and when it did there must have been some doubts in the minds of the town fathers about the legality of following the provisions of a charter whose author was the cause of all the land disputes and that troublesome war with New York. But there was one group who felt very strongly about the matter, and that was the Episcopal Church of Vermont who tried to claim the glebe rights of both the Church of England and the Gospel Society, wherever such provisions had been stipulated. The case went to court with the following result:

> "After recourse to the courts, which was finally decided by the United States Supreme Court, it was decreed that one glebe should revert to the state and the other to the church." (Perry Merrill, *Vermont Under Four Flags*)

Wentworth's allotment of land to the church has been a constant nuisance and complication in many land transactions, and to this day the town of Stratton is required to collect fees from this lease land and turn it over to the Episcopal diocese. (The fees are moderate and apparently are set by the diocese.)

The Church and "Little Stratton"

A church was finally established in Stratton, but it was not the denomination that Governor Wentworth would have preferred. Understandably, any religion related to the Church of England was looked on with great suspicion, especially in view of the fact that the first inhabitants were Congregationalists by inheritance. Hemenway's *Vermont History* has this to say:

> "The early settlers of Stratton were true descendants of the old Puritan stock from which they sprung, and the deep religious sentiment which pervaded their life and character found its legitimate channel in true blue Congregationalism. The Congregational Church of Stratton was organized August 30, 1801, with only nine members."

The church was built mainly through the efforts of this group, and before long the number of parishioners increased considerably. The building, which was also called the Meetinghouse, was erected on the old common near the center of the first and original townsite—known as "Little Stratton." Few people today realize that there ever was such a place, and that remote spot on a foothill will eventually be lost as a landmark in Stratton's early history. Like so many Vermont towns, original settlements shifted their locations, possibly for reasons of accessibility, and eventually "Little Stratton" was abandoned.

The Old Church at the Town of Stratton.

Left behind were all the homes of that beginning settlement, as though an entire community had fled for some unexplained reason. Thirty years ago there were still visible structural signs of those houses—a number were still standing, but tilted and sagging. Today nothing is left but cellar holes and overgrown foundations and the inevitable gravestones.

Probably the most interesting fact connected with this deserted town is that the church was spared from abandonment. What happened is truly a story of Yankee enterprise, because those sturdy citizens took on the unbelievable task of moving that structure down the long hill over a steep, rutted road to its present location. The year was 1849 and in those times it was a remarkable achievement—and one which must have been a labor of love.

It would be incorrect to leave the impression that all people of Stratton remained "true blue" Congregationalists. There were still many who were irked by the church's rigidity, and were rebellious and dissenting. When Vermont began to relax its Sabbath laws the whole region became fertile ground for new and unusual faiths. Stratton was not immune from the itinerant preachers who rode into town, making their bids for lost souls. This brought about an interest in other denominations, and a movement that cut deeply into the old Congregational faith.

Again referring to history, two other denominations were organized and established in the town of Stratton during the nineteenth century. One was the Baptist Society (a faith not held in very high esteem) which had a membership of about forty parishioners in 1825. It is believed that the Baptists and the Congregationalists co-existed very well, although privately they probably denounced each other.

The other denomination that appeared in 1857, was the Free Will Baptists. Not to be confused with the much more conservative Baptist Society. This new religion picked up quite a following, to the dismay of the few remaining "Congos" still living in the area. The Free Will Baptists were often spoken of as that "barrel thumping crowd" because of their loud and fervent approach to salvation. They flourished for quite a number of years, and had the first and only minister to ever live in town, and inhabit the pasonage that was built near the church. Eventually enthusiasm and followers faded away, and the Free Will Baptists were never heard of again.

Somewhere down the years the old meetinghouse returned to its original and proper denomination, the Union Congregational Church. The early records belonging to the church have disappeared—they may exist somewhere, on the other hand they may have been permanently lost or destroyed. The old building still stands at the junction of the roads near the Stratton Town Hall. It is a nice old church, in spite of its lonely and dejected appearance. When you step inside, you step into the past. You are happily surprised to find that the old interior has been kept just as it used to be. It is a pleasant reminder of Stratton's heritage.

A Community Declines

In telling the story of Stratton, we have been briefly touching the edges of its early history. However, there is still one period that should be noted—that sad per -iod after the turn of the century when the community seemed to dwindle away.

Nothing of any great significance seemed to have happened during the last decades of the nineteenth century. The excitement of settlement and growth had long disappeared and now there were no great names or events to attach to the town. No more Daniel Webster speeches, the Big Convention had become ancient history. The original town site had shifted from a hilltop to a lower more accessible spot, and the impossible task of moving the church structure down the long, steep road to its present location had been accomplished. The competition between the Congregationalists and the Free Will Baptists had subsided and the church returned to its original denomination, the Union Congregational Church.

On the national scene the Civil War, with all its fervor, had come and gone, leaving Vermont placid and tranquil—and minus a lot of young men who had decided to live elsewhere. Small communities, like Stratton, showed an alarming downward trend in their census figures. What happened to that "thriving burgh" mentioned by Maria Hemenway in her *Vermont History?* What were the reasons for the decline from which the town never recovered, and the desolation that was the end result? The transition and progress that saved other towns from near extinction never seemed to reach Stratton. By the turn of the century, even the land seemed useless, except for one thing, and that was lumbering.

As is often the case, profits were being made from the misfortune of others. Lumber companies (and a few shrewd individuals) were buying up all available land, and many abandoned lots and farms were acquired by just paying the town the cost of the unpaid taxes. These were the properties of farmers who had toiled for years in order to own a few pitiful acres—finally for one reason or another—having to give up the struggle.

There was now a thick new growth of timberland and this was prompting an invasion of companies interested in the cutting of logs for the pulp mills. This was to become big business on the mountain, but it was of little help to the local people, providing only low type employment.

To the handful of residents still living here the overwhelming logging operations were one more threat to their hopes for the revival of the community. As one old time resident reminisced, "those lumber companies had a strangle hold on the mountain." It must have seemed that way, as day in and day out during the long winter months, the huge loads of logs were hauled down the mountain roads in an endless convoy of horse drawn sleds.

At the height of the operations there were fourteen logging camps all over the mountain, and each camp was given a number by the lumber company who owned and controlled, at that time, most of the land. Gradually, the camps assumed names that either identified their location, such as the "Kendall Farm Camp," or the jobber who had contracted to do the cutting for a particular area, such as the "Dusfresne Job."

Each camp had a cook house, where three meals a day were prepared and served. There were numerous bunk houses for sleeping, and shelters for the work horses. Each camp was a self-sufficient unit. Total workers accommodated per camp were close to forty; ironically the number of people living in the fourteen (or more at certain times) camps exceeded the population of the village of Stratton in its hey-day.

It was a tough life and men had to work extremely hard. It was unremitting hard labor from daybreak until dark. The chain saw had not been invented and cutting was done with the two man cross-cut saw. Often one man was faster and stronger on his end of the saw, and this would lead to short tempers and disputes. This was all part of living and working six days a week, and sometimes seven, in a lumber camp—and it was a way of life on Stratton Mountain for many, many years.

To illustrate to what extent the lumber companies controlled the acreage on the mountain, the following information is on record in the town clerk's office:

> "Beginning in October 1919, Champlain Realty Company began acquiring lands already held by half dozen or more logging and lumber companies, as well as individuals, and disposed of all to American Realty, on April 11, 1934."

This represents a fifteen year period when one company was in control of most of the lumbering on Stratton. A rather frightening situation to those who still were residents.

After that American Realty continued operations for six years, but "merged with International Paper on June 28, 1940." According to the town clerk's records, International Paper is still the largest land owner in the town of Stratton, presently holding title to slightly more than fifty percent of the land. (Stratton comprises an area of nearly 29,000 acres.)

At this point there were few remaining families who still lived and voted in the community, and by necessity they fitted themselves to a stark pattern of life. There weren't many choices for gainful employment except working for one of the lumber companies—a dreary existence with little to look forward to. Perhaps for the men, one of their few pleasures came from the prime hunting and fishing that the mountain still provided, and which in turn put much needed meat and fish on the family table. Sadly, it was also at this point in time when the black bear population was nearly decimated, not only by the natives but by the "alien" hunters as well. The cruel practice of massive bear hunts had been going on for years, even the slaughter of small cubs and their mothers was an accepted pastime. It was 1950 before the legislature finally realized that something had to be done and placed a closed season for a few years on the black bear in order to save them from extinction.

That was the status of Stratton for nearly forty years. To those who lived in the neighboring towns, Stratton was called a "no man's land," a place where people had come and struggled for years, and then went away—for good! It was almost as though it was a closed little world, a beautiful and frightening wilderness existing for lumbermen and hunters. But there were going to be changes and by a strange coincidence one of these lumbermen would be marked by destiny to play an incredibly important role in what was going to happen to this mountain.

Vermont loggers at the turn of the century.

Herbert "Tink" Smith

As it turned out, it was Tink Smith who would become the Stratton lumberman "marked by destiny" to become one of the principal characters in this story. Those were the years of the 40's and Tink and his brother, Nelson "Dick" Smith, would have laughed if someone had ever suggested that the spot where they were logging would someday be the base area and the parking lot for thousands of skiing patrons.

Herbert "Tink" Smith

Tink Smith was born in South Londonderry, Vermont, on September 8, 1915, the youngest child of Nelson B. and Hattie Landfear Smith. As was the custom, he was born at home and the presiding physician was a Dr. Mellington, who apparently forgot to officially record the birth in the town records. This error was discovered some years later when Tink applied for his passport and was told there was no record of his ever having been born. Somehow the matter was rectified and Tink was eventually issued a passport.

As a youngster he attended the local schools in South Londonderry; later he went to Leland and Gray Seminary in Townshend, Vermont. His classmates remember him as a quiet, shy student who often blushed glowingly when called upon by the instructor; a characteristic he long ago overcame. When he was a senior his family moved to Richford, Vermont, and it was there he completed his high school education.

The following is from an article written by Jeff Dickson in the *Mountain News,* November 23, 1973:

> "In the early 1920's Tink Smith went to work in his father's lumber mill at South Londonderry. The mill was a small, hardwood dimension mill where wooden penholders were made out of white birch and basswood. The work was not easy for a 10-year old, but Tink enjoyed it. During the Depression, Tink's father left southern Vermont to open a mill at Richford, near the Canadian border. There Tink worked 10 hours a day during his school vacations and was paid $10 a week. But when the mill burned in 1933, the Smith family moved back to South Londonderry to start anew, purchasing stumpage from IP (on Stratton Mountain) and hauling the pulp and chip wood from sawmill slabs. The new mill was a family operation, and has been ever since."

That is how it all started for the Smith family and their involvement with lumbering on Stratton Mountain—just a small logging operation many years ago, that little by little became a real business with considerable land holdings, and on a mountain with a very special future.

With the onset of World War II there was increased demand for lumber, and by 1942 Tink and his brother had four portable sawmills on the mountain. This required a payroll of nearly 100 men who worked in one capacity or another, doing the various jobs needed for taking the logs from stump to sawmill. The portable sawmill has practically gone out of popular use today, but years ago it was almost a necessity to set up a mill near the particular section of timberland that was being logged, and later be able to move it easily to another location when it was needed. Today, with improved motorized vehicles for use in the woods, along with the powerful trucks to haul the logs to the stationary or permanent mills, there is little use for the portable mill. Tink talked, almost wistfully, about the pleasant humming sounds of a small mill set up in the deep woods, and the rapport that existed between the men running that mill—a scene that has now faded from the Vermont picture.

When the Smith family started their operations on Stratton, the big companies, or their jobbers, were still controlling much of what happened on that mountain, including the general welfare of their employees; unfortunately, showing only a casual consideration in that area. Ten and 12-hour work days were the rule and not the exception, and minimum wage and overtime were unheard of. Sick leave, often due to injury on the job, was also unheard of, and any financial help from the lumber companies was minimal.

But if you worked for Smith, Inc., as the business was now called, things were different. The Smiths seemed to do more for their workers, and this evidence of social responsibility gave them the reputation of being good employers. Both men felt an obligation to their help and their families.

Not only did they start and maintain a bonus fund, but, if for some reason a worker and his family needed food and other necessities, they were provided without question. And, in a real emergency help was always available. Such were some of the qualities that Tink was and is best known for. A hearty and friendly man, the Vermont workmen liked and trusted him.

It was not until 1950 that an accelerated interest in Vermont mountains and Vermont winters came about. Mount Snow had opened and was billed as "the largest ski resort in the world." On any big weekend you could see thousands of skiers on its slopes. Suddenly, there were people who were looking around for mountains, with development in mind. Snow, which to the native used to be something shoveled or avoided, was now an asset. Particularly to a new type of visitor that was arriving in increasing numbers—the skier. To Tink and his brother it was a pleasant surprise that their land on the mountain had become such a desirable location for a ski area.

Tink always had his share of the tight, bargaining instincts of the true Vermonter, whether he was swapping acreage or forming a company to utilize sawdust. He had been approached before about the land, and both groups who had approached him were interested in building a ski resort. But he wasn't ready for a commitment. He was a canny woodsman, and, until he could see the clear outline of a satisfactory deal he hung back. It was Frank Snyder whose ideas appealed the most to Tink, when they finally met. It wasn't long after that Tink decided to throw in his lot with Frank, and he did so with energy and enthusiasm.

In the course of the planned development of the mountain, a personal dream was also fulfilled for him since the plans included a non-sectarian chapel. Today, the Chapel of the Snows, located within walking distance of the Stratton base lodge, welcomes worshippers of all faiths. Tink deserves the credit for this accomplishment.

Tink is married to the former Catherine (Kay) Gildea from North Andover, Massachusetts. When Kay graduated from "Normal School" her first position was in the hamlet of Rawsonville. It didn't take long for Tink to discover the attractive little Irish schoolteacher, and he was soon squiring her to square dances and putting on her skates. She was "Tink's girl," and he married her two short years after they met.

As Tink moved into the planning of Stratton, Kay also took an active part, discovering things to do that no one else seemed to think of. She supported and became actively involved in the establishment of church services, first in the second floor dining room of the base lodge (which during big weekends became so crowded that it was difficult to tell the worshippers from the diners), and, when the time came, in planning the services of the Chapel of the Snows. It was Kay Smith who was responsible for naming the Chapel—a beautiful name that is so appropriate. For many years Kay has been associated with the Stratton Arts Festival as one of the founders, as a trustee, and for several years as president.

If one looks back to the time when Frank Snyder and Tink Smith met, one can only say that it was a most unlikely combination—the city boy and the country boy. Tink's first impression of Frank, after hours of nervously waiting for Frank and Jessie to find their way out of the Stratton woods in the pitch black of the night, was that he must be some sort of a fool. No man in his right mind would start up a strange mountain, with his wife, in the afternoon of a cool October day with the distinct possibility that total darkness would set in before they ever reached the top! As Tink said, "Better men than Frank Snyder have been lost for days on that Mountain."

When it was nearly midnight, Tink decided that the time had come to call in help to hunt for the Snyders, when suddenly they emerged from the woods, none the worse for the experience, but possibly a great deal wiser. Tink was relieved, but probably had to use a lot of self-control to keep from giving them an old-fashioned lecture.

Later on when asked about that first meeting with Frank, Tink's comment was, "Even with him doing that dumb thing, I liked him immediately. I wasn't leery of him at all. We had a good working relationship most of those early years. We had a good time too, and nobody can take that away. But most of all I am pleased and proud we got this far." That's how Tink tells it—with a typical good natured chuckle and another puff on the ever-present El Producto.

N
S

Images of Vermont

The Stratton Story

Frank Snyder first became aware of Stratton Mountain on Sunday, February 1, 1959. He and his wife, Jessie, were returning from a visit to The Foster Place, a small inn in Stowe, Vermont, where they had first met in 1948.[1]

Although skiing had been terrible (sheet ice, according to Jessie's diary), they had enjoyed being with old friends. Now, they were making the drive back to their home in Greenwich, Connecticut. It was a long trip over narrow roads and would take seven hours. As they passed through Dorset on Route 7, Snyder commented that this drive from Stowe was really too long—particularly now that they had children. Why, he mused, hadn't anyone ever built a ski area in southern Vermont?[2] These looked like pretty big mountains. He pulled out a road map and began studying it. There were a number of 3,000-foot peaks: Dorset, which they were just passing and, beyond it, Mt. Equinox, rising over 3,800 feet. Farther west was an even bigger mountain called Stratton, with a summit elevation of 3,936 feet. Whereas all the other mountains were bordered by state highways, Stratton Mountain seemed to be isolated in a huge wilderness area labeled "National Forest."

Snyder put the map away. Returning to the city, he forgot about skiing and Vermont mountains, as he concentrated once again on the problems of earning a living.

Three months later, he had a lunch date with Henry Homes (brother of Dr. Robert Homes, who is today Stratton Mountain's doctor-in-residence). The subject of skiing came up. Henry had also spent a week at Stowe in February. Both agreed that the long drive from New York made weekend skiing at Stowe almost impossible. Remembering the road map, Snyder put a question to Homes: why hadn't anyone ever developed one of the big mountains in southern Vermont?

"You know," Homes replied, "I had a ski instructor at Stowe who mentioned that he is very interested in doing just that! I can't remember the mountain's name, but the ski instructor claimed he has already put an investor group together."

After the luncheon, the subject was forgotten again, until Homes telephoned Snyder in mid-July. "Do you remember back in May, when I said there's a Stowe ski instructor interested in building a new ski area in southern Vermont?"

Snyder said that he did.

"Well, the name of the mountain is Stratton. The ski instructor is Bob Wright. I hope you don't mind that I gave him your name, because he's sitting here in my office with a model of the mountain, and he wants to call on you."

Snyder told Homes to send him down. That afternoon, Robert Dudley Wright walked into the Moore & Munger offices in downtown New York. A tall, good-looking man in his late twenties, Wright had been a successful amateur racer. He had gone into education, had married and fathered six children, and was then teaching at Norwich University, near Northfield, Vermont.

Speaking quietly and slowly, Wright explained the reasons why he felt Stratton could be an outstanding ski mountain. First of all, it was high—the highest mountain in southern Vermont—and the seventh highest in the state. It would be possible to ski off the summit, he said, whereas, at Stowe, the

[1] The Foster Place was one of the oldest and most famous small winter inns in New England. Founded by Jane Nichols and Ann Thomas in 1940, its charm was its simplicity—a plain clapboard house without central heat, where the guests helped set the tables and washed the dishes, and where a whole generation of Boston and New York young people learned to love this way of life. It closed in 1975.

[2] Actually there were large ski areas in southern Vermont; Bromley and Mt. Snow, but Snyder was not aware of the fact at that time.

top 500 feet of vertical is solid rock and will never be skiable.

"And," Wright added, "Stratton Mountain is in the middle of the snowbelt."

"What is the snowbelt?" asked Snyder.

Wright explained that it is the name commonly given by meteorologists to the narrow strip of land that gets the heaviest snowfall in the state. It runs north and south the length of Vermont, extending only five miles or so east and west of the central ridge of mountains. Stratton is right in this belt. Dorset Peak and Mt. Equinox, although almost as high, are well to the west of the snowbelt and therefore receive less than half as much snow.

"There's another peculiarity about the snowfall in southern Vermont that the northerners don't understand," Wright pointed out. "Stowe's slogan is: 'There's always snow in Stowe,' and it does get a little more snow than southern Vermont. But the snow is mostly very light and dry stuff coming off the Great Lakes and is usually followed by northwest winds that blow it right off the trails."

"Southern Vermont," he continued to explain, "gets more of its snow from the coastal storms—the nor'easters that drop *heavy* accumulations of wetter snow. This kind sticks to the slopes, does not blow away, and it stands up to the skier wear better."

At this point, Wright turned to a small cardboard box, which he had carried into the office with him. From it he took a scale model of Stratton Mountain—about 18 inches long on each side and painted green, with a trail network done in white.

"This is a mountain for intermediate skiers," Wright went on, "but it has some advanced terrain on the north side, down this gully, where the descent is steep enough to give anyone a thrill."

Snyder plunged right into economics: "How much money is needed to develop this mountain and get into business?"

"About $400,000."

"How much are you looking for from each individual investor?"

"We're hoping for $10,000."

"With 50% debt, that means $200,000, and twenty investors—a big undertaking. How many do you now have?"

Wright admitted that no one had signed up yet.

"Well, who comprises your group?"

Seven people had shown interest, Wright indicated, all but one of them Vermonters. The best known was Pearl Buck, the famous novelist who owned about 300 acres facing the mountain. Others were: George Breen, Pearl Buck's business manager in Vermont; Malvine Cole, another summer resident and neighbor of Miss Buck; Tink Smith, a local lumberman; and A. Luke Crispe, an attorney in Brattleboro. The lone out-of-stater was Grant Hubley, who lived in New York. Hubley was a salesman for Homestake Oil Company and had been helpful in supplying names of potential investors. The Vermonters had each contributed $500 to fund expenses.

Wright now asked if Snyder was interested in investing.

"Yes, I'm interested. I'll put up $10,000, but only if you find another twenty people who will do the same."

The meeting over, Wright went away a happy man. He had found his first investor.

Commitment to the Mountain

August rolled around and, with it, vacation time. The Snyders went off on a pack trip in the Sierra Nevada Mountains, while Bob Wright plugged away in New York, searching for twenty investors.

When Snyder and Wright met again in September, Wright was discouraged. He had labored for two months, following up on every name that he could uncover. With the exception of Snyder, he had struck out everywhere.

This news came as no surprise to Snyder. While he knew nothing about ski area development, 12 years of law practice and business experience led him to question the chances of such an effort. He had already sized up Wright as a pleasant man (a good skier, and maybe a good teacher), but a novice in business affairs. His so-called "Vermont group" appeared to be either unwilling or unable to finance a project of this scope. It was going to take much more than $3,000 expense money to launch a major ski area.

Snyder was reluctant to become involved beyond his initial offer to invest. The prudent thing to do would be to tell Wright to give up and say goodbye. On the other hand, his curiosity had been aroused. Apparently, this was no common mountain. Not only was it the highest in southern Vermont and received more snow than almost anywhere else in the East; also, it was only a four-hour drive from his home in Connecticut. What a perfect place for the Snyder children to learn to ski!

It was a difficult moment. Wright was desperate, his year-long dream dissolving. Reluctant to turn him away completely, Snyder invited him to drive out to his home that night to talk some more.

Snyder felt that it should be possible to sell 20 investors on putting up $10,000 to $20,000 each, if they were offered a fair amount of equity through a good prospectus. He felt that Wright had been ineffective through no fault of his own because of inexperience and because the necessary groundwork had not been done. It was clear that, if the project were to get off the ground, everything would have to be re-studied. Costs would have to be re-estimated and the numbers re-done. Vermont would have to be reconnoitered to find out what investor support was there and what land was available for sale. The Mountain would have to be climbed every day during the coming winter to work out the trail system. An accountant would have to be hired to refine the numbers. Most important of all, other local promoters had to be lined up.

Wright was willing—even eager—to plunge ahead. He was ready to resign his job, but he would need financial help.

It was at this precise moment that Snyder committed himself to Stratton. He agreed to pay Wright the equivalent of his university salary until June 1960—$890 per month, plus expenses. The understanding was that Wright would keep his family in Northfield until a house could be found in the Stratton area. He would shuttle between Northfield and Greenwich, working for Snyder on the prospectus, on land purchases, and on trail layout.

The conversation went on into the early hours of a new day. As the fire died down in the Snyders' big fireplace, the two men shook hands on the arrangement, and the next morning, Wright left for Vermont to submit his resignation and to give the news to his wife. A new chapter in the saga of Stratton was about to begin.

Drafting the Prospectus

The prospectus should be a selling document, Snyder felt. It should exhibit a lot of expertise, while presenting a logical and reasonably thorough plan for development. This meant that major problems should be identified and dealt with knowledgeably. As in all prospectuses, there should be sections on competition, on capital budgets, pro forma operating statements, and a proposed capital structure.

Snyder realized that he was going to have to do much of the drafting, but, at the same time, he felt that he could not spare time from his business responsibilities at Moore & Munger during working hours. So most of the background would have to be supplied by Wright, with Snyder reviewing the progress during evenings and weekends.

Like most recreational skiers, Snyder had almost no knowledge of how ski resorts are built or operated. Wright was not much better informed, but, at least, he had worked at Stowe and had observed other New England areas during his racing years. It was a case of the blind leading the blind, but they worked hard at it. Evenings at the Snyder residence now consisted of extended grilling sessions, with Snyder questioning Wright on every phase of the business. Notes were taken. Where both men lacked information, Wright was instructed to make phone calls, or, one way or another, to find out more facts.

The major problems were identified. First, and most important, was the question of an access road. The future base area was four miles from the small town of Bondville. A good paved highway would have to be built. Would the State put up any money? Second, the land was not owned by the U.S. Forest Service, as all maps showed, but instead was owned by the International Paper Company. Complicating this was the fact that 400 acres of the summit was owned by a competing company—St. Regis Paper. Would they lease, and how could negotiations begin? What about lifts? Who made them and what did they cost? How were trails built and how much did they cost? Where could a trail consultant be found? What about a base lodge? An architect had to be located. What about competition? The more they researched—the deeper they dug—the more problems they unearthed.

On Saturday, October 3, Frank and Jessie Snyder drove to Manchester to see Stratton Mountain for the first time and to become acquainted with the "Vermont Group." Meeting Bob Wright in Manchester, they drove over to Bondville, leaving the car at Malvine Cole's little house on the Mountain (not far from the present Stratton Golf Academy).

At 2:30 PM, they started up the trail. Hiking past "Forest Haunt," Pearl Buck's stone guest cottage, they soon came onto a large beaver pond known as Orcutt Meadows (long since replaced by the Stratton Golf Course lake). From here, they climbed straight uphill to a swampy bowl (now the base area), then along an overgrown logging road curving up past what is now the Snow Bowl.

It was 4:30 PM when the climbers finally bushwacked through spruce trees to the summit. No time wasted there, they immediately started the descent. The downward trek was slow in the gathering darkness, with no flashlight to guide them. But, by keeping the sound of Styles Brook on their left, they were able to find the old jeep road to North Cemetery (now the Sun Bowl cross-country trail), and, at 11:30 PM they walked into Malvine Cole's cottage. She had become worried about their absence and had phoned Tink Smith, who had immediately driven over.

It was the first time that Snyder and Smith had met. Perhaps neither was very impressed with the other. Tink was just about to call out some of his loggers to go up and find the city slickers. Smiling, he told them so, in a steady, unbroken monologue, with cigar in mouth. Snyder simply couldn't understand what Tink was saying. The burly red-faced Vermonter seemed to be jolly and full of good humor, but only one word in three was comprehensible. Only later, did he come to realize that this merry woodsman talked just as fast as he thought and was a lot shrewder than he appeared.

The Vermont Group

The routine that had been established in September continued: long overnight visits by Bob Wright to the Snyder home, during which the prospectus was worked over and over; weekend forays to Vermont to look at properties and to meet the members of the "Vermont group"; conferences in New York with accountants and consultants.

But in spite of all the activity and even though some good properties were being acquired, all was not going well. For one thing, the "Vermont Group" wasn't a group at all. It was becoming apparent that, of the five people Wright[3] had named, few would contribute much effort. Snyder was unable to get through to Pearl Buck, who had moved back to her winter home in Buck's County, Pennsylvania.

Several people felt that Malvine Cole was the "Mother of Stratton." It had been her idea, to build a ski area on Stratton Mountain and to bring Bob Wright down from Stowe. She was anxious to help any way she could.

Tink Smith was a different situation. He was eager to build Stratton, but he had doubts about Wright and hadn't made up his mind yet about Snyder. He felt that he had all the aces himself. He owned land on Stratton, did much of International Paper's and St. Regis' lumbering. He was confident his friends at International Paper and St. Regis would never lease Stratton Mountain to Snyder or anyone else, if he chose to oppose them. So, in good Vermont fashion, he sat back, watching and waiting.

Wright, meanwhile was having problems in Vermont. Unfortunately, through no fault of his own, he missed by one day putting a bid on 255 acres of counterslope land on the Mountain, land which was owned by Edward Scheier and was for sale at $40,-000.

More disturbing was the fact that Snyder's old skiing friends were showing no desire to put any money into Stratton. Over and over, he was to be turned down. The words were always different, but the message was the same:

"No thanks. Don't ask me to invest in a ski area—they just don't make money. But the idea sounds great, so hurry up and build it. I promise to ski there."

[3] It is also understood that in addition there was a Mr. R. Pickett and a Dr. Arnold who were part of this group.

The Community Concept

Snyder was now using every spare minute to contact friends and acquaintances, setting up lunch dates and sometimes calling on them at their homes or offices. More and more, he was finding the Stratton project crowding in on his regular office responsibilities. And, more and more, he was realizing that, without a good prospectus, he was not going to get anywhere. Work continued steadily on the "memorandum." The discipline of reducing thoughts to paper was slowly bringing the Stratton project together. It was beginning to be clear, for instance, that a resort built on Stratton Mountain would have one important advantage over all existing ski areas in Vermont: it would be built on private land. Stowe, Killington, and Sugarbush were on state or Federal lands, and government policy prohibited construction of private homes and buildings. At Stratton, it would be possible to integrate village, chalets, lift, and ski slopes in a planned and logical way—something new in Vermont. Instead of building a drive-in, drive-out day ski area, they would create a resort community on Stratton Mountain.

Snyder drove over to Tink Smith's house on November 29 to bring him up to date on the "memorandum" and to talk about the village concept. Smith listened politely. He wasn't a skier and never would be. He was a golfer, and his private dream was to build a golf course. However, both men hit it off pretty well in this second meeting. Tink's ideas and Frank's both went into the memorandum, with the result that probably for the first time in the United States, a development plan was published which joined a major ski area with contiguous golf course, village, and residential areas.

To dream up the concept was one thing. To organize the financing was turning out to be quite another. November slipped by without any new investors, while the estimates of capital costs rose steadily. Bob Wright's original $400,000 was now $800,000, which meant that they would have to raise $400,000 of equity capital. If each investor unit included $10,000 of stock, they would have to sell 40 units.

Nevertheless, there was one positive development. Malvine Cole had contacted one of the Windham County State Legislators, Bob Gannett of Brattleboro, suggesting that he might want to meet with the Stratton Mountain principals, and Gannett had courteously agreed. The meeting turned out to be a success. It was clear to Bob Gannett that the Snyders were responsible people with financial muscle, and he agreed to throw his support behind the project. One of the most serious problems, they all agreed, was going to be an access road from Bondville up the four miles of forest and mountainside to the proposed base area.

Gannett pointed out that the State had long had a policy of encouraging private investment in ski areas through the funding of access roads. A bill had just been enacted to provide a five-mile access road at Killington. The same should be possible at Stratton.

But there were practical problems. All the local legislators must be approached and informed. The Stratton Group would have to prove that it had the financial wherewithal to go through with the project. There were other hopeful developers in the state seeking money—a Swiss by the name of Hans Thorner had just announced that he was going to build a ski area on Glebe Mountain in Londonderry. He was going to call it "Magic Mountain," and he was already lobbying for a road. Finally, there might be opposition in Montpelier, because $1 million had already been appropriated for this purpose over the last two years.

The legislature would be meeting in January, 1960. The bill would have to go into the hopper immediately. The session would be over in March or April. The timing was wrong, Gannett concluded. It would be premature to try for a bill in the 1960 legislature. Better to wait a year. By then, the Stratton project would be well on its way, and they would have had time to convince the legislators that they should support it. At the same time, it wasn't too early to start lobbying efforts, he said, and he agreed to organize a meeting of Windham County Representatives before the current session began. Snyder said he would have the memorandum ready for them in three weeks. Consequently, December 14 was set as the date, and the Colburn House in Manchester the place for a Vermont legislator dinner.

Stratton Mountain Is Launched!

The next three weeks were feverishly busy. With the help of John Stookey, a business consultant, they reviewed the financial data and rewrote sections of the text. On December 7, the manuscript was sent off to the printer, where 100 numbered copies were run off and bound. During that week, Malvine Cole sent out invitations to all legislators in southern Vermont.

The response was encouraging. Thirty-four Representatives accepted. Then Snyder received a telephone call from Windham County's other State Senator, Edward G. Janeway.

"Here I have been one of the biggest supporters for ski areas in the Senate, and I didn't know that a major effort was underway in my own back yard at Stratton. I'll be delighted to give you every bit of support I can."

Snyder hadn't met Senator Janeway face to face yet, but this telephone call was to initiate a business association, as well as a long and deep friendship with one of Vermont's most outstanding citizens.

As to the memorandum, Snyder felt that it should reflect careful and solid thinking. For starters, they should try to give some impression of organization and commitment by incorporating. So, a New York company was formed, styled "Stratton Mountain Corporation," and Snyder funded it with $10,000 cash. Since his Moore & Munger Partnership Agreement prohibited him from serving as an officer of another company, he set up Bob Wright as president.

The new Stratton Mountain Corporation played host at the Colburn House dinner. Turn-out was excellent. Tink Smith and Ed Janeway attended, marking the first public appearance of the three men, who, together, were to guide Stratton over the coming decades. After cocktails and dinner, Bob Gannett rose to say a few words in favor of the project and to point out the importance of a state-financed access road.

The party broke up early, guests thanking hosts politely but giving no hint of how they felt about backing a road bill. Whether such a road was in their future or not was unclear to the promoters that night. But one thing was certain: Stratton Mountain had been launched!

Euphoria in Vermont was quickly followed by gloom in New York. In the two weeks before Christmas, Snyder distributed copies of the memorandum to a selected group of prospects. Wright came down from Vermont, and together they called on every one of them. Not a glimmer of investor interest could be stirred. The low point in the whole Stratton saga came when Snyder got a turn-down from Stan Rumbough on December 21. Stan was an old Foster Place skier and one-time member of the Yale Ski Team. Not only was he wealthy, handsome, and wedded to the beautiful Dina Hutton (now Dina Merrill), but also he was a close friend of Grant Hubley's. If they couldn't sell Stan, they really didn't have much to sell, Snyder thought, as they stood on the sidewalk outside of Stan's office building on that gloomy afternoon, four days before Christmas.

He hadn't been able to find a single person in all of New York who would join him. A lot of New York people were ready to go along for the ride, but no one had stood up with hard cash. The same seemed true in Vermont.

December 22 brought a snowstorm and a white

Christmas in the New York area. Over the long holiday weekend, Snyder pondered: Why couldn't he and Wright raise money? Were they going about it wrong? Perhaps the whole idea was mad. Should it be forgotten?

Once again, he had the urge to throw in the towel and tell Wright to forget about Stratton Mountain. After all, everything seemed to be against them. They didn't know how to promote the financing of a new company. They didn't really have one. Sure, he'd put up $10,000 and formed Stratton Mountain Corporation, but it was a shell. There was nothing visible—no existing facilities, no trails, no base lodge, no organization, and no track record. Stratton was still nothing but an idea, a dream. They really hadn't made any progress at all.

The Principals Go It Alone

How, Snyder wondered, do you get people to invest their hard-earned money in a new, untested idea? He had tried to follow the example set by Lowell Thomas and Roland Palmedo in 1941, when they had put together a syndicate to build the chair lift at Stowe—the first chair lift ever built in New England. But those gentlemen had had a lot going for them: they were well known, with a large circle of friends; and Stowe actually *existed*—the trails had already been skied on for several seasons. Perhaps here was the key. Perhaps if they built trails first, and *then* tried to raise money—they might be successful.

On January 2, Snyder loaded his family into their old station wagon for a three-day visit to Vermont. On the drive up, he made two New Year's resolutions: (1) Since he had failed to find a single partner in New York, he would make a final effort to build the Stratton ski area by offering to throw in his lot with the only two people he had met in Vermont who were heavyweights and appeared to be really dedicated to the idea: Tink Smith and Ed Janeway. If they were ready to roll the dice with him, he would join them; (2) He would propose that, together, they would go it alone, until they had built something visible that would convince the public—and potential investors—that the Stratton Mountain development was a reality. This meant risking a lot more money than he had ever bargained for, but there was simply no other way. It was either go it alone with Smith and Janeway, or drop the whole idea.

It rained heavily on that 1960 New Year's weekend. Deluges fell on January 3, washing out most New England ski areas. But, if this was bad news for Vermont's ski area operators, it marked a new beginning for Stratton Mountain. The three men who were to form a new company—Ed Janeway, Tink Smith, and Frank Snyder—agreed on that day to establish a Vermont Corporation and to negotiate leases from International and St. Regis Paper Companies. They also agreed that they would build a work road into the base area so they could clear trails next summer, and all the world would see that a new ski area was coming. They would complete these developments alone. Then, and only then would they sign up investors.

That afternoon, the three drove to Rutland to visit Governor Bob Stafford at his home. Stafford was a skier, and he quickly agreed to put his influence behind the new development. His help was to count for much over the coming months.

Although the three men probably didn't realize it at the time, a triumvirate had been fashioned—a combination of energy, experience, dedication, and reputation that would be hard to beat anywhere in the ski business.

Each brought different strengths. At 38, Snyder was the youngest. He was the experienced skier who had visited many of the major resorts in the United States and Europe over the last 20 years. He was a natural leader, and his legal and business background would be of critical importance in organizing, planning, and financing the new company.

Smith brought unbelievable energy and enthusiasm. In many ways the quintessential Vermonter, he could repair anything. And there was nothing that he was afraid to try. Nicknamed "Tinker" years before, he could fix a bulldozer, or drive it. He knew every foot of Stratton Mountain. There was never a doubt in his mind that the project could and would be built. He just couldn't wait to get up on that mountain and get started with the job.

Janeway was to be the diplomat who accomplished more than either of his partners in the early months. Oldest, most experienced, and with the coolest head of the three, he was to be the one who, working quietly in the background, was to bring the community behind the project and who, in the end, was to be Stratton's best salesman.

Within days, two others joined them: Nelson "Dick" Smith, brother of Tink, and Luke Crispe, their Vermont attorney. These were the five men who, assisted first by Bob Wright and later by Elmer Argast, were the founders and builders of Stratton.

Beyond the spirit of friendship that was to grow and to build this diverse group together over the years was a powerful dedication—a determination that still exists twenty years later—to build the finest winter resort in all of New England. This was the driving force that was to carry them through many struggles and over all obstacles during the next two decades.

Surveying the Competition

Snyder had come up with the idea of making a survey of the competition, and, in that winter of 1959/1960, he visited all of Vermont's major ski areas. The object was to study their business operations, but he had other reasons: to meet the people who had built them and were operating them; to get the word around that a Stratton Mountain project really was underway, and to look for talent. Stratton was going to need many good people. Some were going to have to come from competing resorts.

On January 16, he went over to Bromley to meet its founder and owner, Fred Pabst. Fred was one of the earliest American ski pioneers. He had been a jumper in the 1920's, competing here and in Europe. He had gotten into ski area operation in the 1930's, and soon had six different areas running in Vermont and Wisconsin. When he built Bromley in 1936, it was the second ski area to open in the United States with uphill transportation (the first being Suicide Six in Woodstock, Vermont).

Any session with Fred was an experience. Handsome and an imposing six-feet-four inches tall, he had lived just the kind of independent career that suited his forthright and outspoken character. He called it the way he saw it, and couldn't care less if he hurt feelings along the way. At the same time, nobody was ever more generous or hospitable.

On the top floor of his converted red farmhouse-office, he had installed a panelled *sanctum sanctorum* with recessed bar and windows that looked out over the base area. This is where he loved to entertain visitors.

Over a late morning highball, Fred steered Frank to the window, while pointing out some of Bromley's features. Every slope had been groomed and seeded with grass, so that they were skiable with only four inches of snow. This was his innovation, Fred said, and very few ski areas had followed his lead yet. But he was proudest of the J-Bar lifts, which he had invented and which he claimed were the best and safest lifts in the world. T-Bars were much inferior, he said, because they rotated under the skier and tended to dump beginners. He had put up one double chair lift, and he had to admit that his customers preferred it to the J-Bars, simply because it was faster, but to his dying day, he would never alter his conviction that the J-Bars were his greatest contribution to the sport of skiing.

As they stood at the window, they could see Stratton Mountain eight miles away. It was a very cold day, with a strong northwest wind blowing clouds across its summit.

"Stratton will have good skiing if you can get a road into it, but it's going to be cold and windy over there," Fred said. "I don't worry about your competition. People ski here because they like the warm sun. They'll never leave Bromley to ski Stratton."

He did worry, though, about the competition for beds.

"There just aren't enough inns in this valley. If new ski areas are going to be built on Stratton and Magic Mountains, then we are going to have a problem with accommodation."

It was a cordial interview. Whatever misgivings he may have had about the impending competition, Fred Pabst would be friendly and helpful to the neophytes across the way.

The next day, Snyder visited Mount Snow and was introduced to mass skiing, southern Vermont style. After the New Year's rain, two nice snowstorms had laid down some really fine conditions. Streams of cars were now moving up Route 100 from West Dover, and the huge parking lots were rapidly filling up. Snyder had never seen such hordes of skiers.

In the Mount Snow office, he met their new general manager, Win Lauder. Win was a young escapee from Greenwich, Connecticut. A few years ago, he had built an inn at Mt. Snow, and now the banks had convinced Mt. Snow's flamboyant absentee owner, Walt Schoenknecht, to install Win as full time boss. Bright, good-looking, and just as outspoken as Fred Pabst, Win laughed at Frank's comment about the crowds of skiers engulfing the area.

"Yes," he said, "there probably will be 5,000 skiers in the area today. But Walt likes to exaggerate, so the news release will probably claim 10,000."

Then they went up the Mountain. No lifts anywhere could compare with Mt. Snow's. All others were true aerial lifts, while Mt. Snow's were modified freight conveyors. There were no big towers or heavy cables. Instead, chain-link belts supported the chairs and were hauled over rollers. The whole thing clanked dreadfully and dropped grease on the passengers. But they did transport a lot of people—an incredible 1,200 skiers per hour on each lift. There was no doubt that Mr. Snow was handling the crowds well that day. The snow conditions were excellent, and it was surprisingly warm—warmer than the day before at Bromley.

Win was amused that Frank was planning a ski area on Stratton Mountain.

"Why in God's name do you want to do that?" he asked. "Building and running a ski area is a hell of a job. Believe me, you'll never see a pay-out and you'll sweat bullets trying."

Here was the question again. Why does anyone ever build a ski resort?

On the weekend of February 6 and 7, Snyder

drove north to Sugarbush, which he had never seen before, and met Founder and President Damon Gadd.

Damon was a New Yorker and a Yale graduate. Although he hadn't skied for very long, he was widely traveled, and it was his dream to make Sugarbush into a great international resort. He was now into his third season, and the development was showing some signs of fulfilling his objectives.

His first innovation was to build a gondola to the summit. It was a new design by De Savio and Carlevaro of Turin, Italy. Brightly painted cars whisked skiers up an 11,000-foot lift line to the summit of Mt. Lincoln in less than 15 minutes. Two chair lifts completed the lift system.

The mountain conformation was interesting—a giant bowl, with lifts fanning out from a single base area. It was the reverse of Stratton Mountain, where there would be several base areas and where the lifts would tend to converge on the summit.

Damon had purchased land along his access road, and, although the lifts were in National Forest, his base lodge and base area were on company land. His plan was to build a village with shops and apartments within walking distance of the lifts.

He was a sophisticated thinker, and he had already brought Sugarbush several steps away from the old New England concept of red galluses and frost-bitten noses. It was the place to go in 1961, if you were looking for international flavor. If Mt. Snow was sometimes overrun by busloads from Brooklyn and Queens and Bromley catered only to older skiers who loved sunny slopes and didn't take their skiing too seriously, then Sugarbush was the home of the new "Jet Set." Boeing 707's were just now beginning to fly from New York to Europe, cutting the flight time from sixteen hours to six. Those good-looking, well-dressed Sugarbush skiers could just be returning from Courchevel, St. Anton, or Davos; and, for that reason, Sugarbush was soon to be nicknamed "Mascara Mountain."

Both Frank Snyder and Bob Wright went for a look around the Mountain. The ride up the gondola was fast and comfortable, but Wright maintained that it was a bad lift for the stockholders. It could carry only 600 skiers an hour, less than half the capacity of one of Mt. Snow's clunkers, and it probably cost four times as much to build and run.

From Sugarbush, they went over to Killington, which had opened a year earlier. A five-mile access road had been constructed through unbroken forest to a state-owned base lodge. Killington's founder, Preston Smith, had not only extracted a road from the state, he had also talked them into building a base facility. Killington Peak is State Forest, as is Mt. Mansfield, and State policy called for more support than developments to be built on private or U.S. Forest land.

Compared to Sugarbush, Killington had a very unfinished appearance. The double chair was unpainted; debris was lying around. Wright was contemptuous: "a bunch of amateurs," he mumbled. He saw little else than disaster and bankruptcy here. How wrong he turned out to be! But, in 1960, Killington was the least impressive of all the areas they visited.

No market survey could be complete without a visit to Stowe, the self-proclaimed "Ski Capitol of the East." This is where Snyder had skied when attending college, and a visit was always something like a homecoming.

Stowe's president and general manager was Sepp Ruschp, who, like Fred Pabst, was one of the early ski pioneers. He had been a sensational amateur racer in his native Austria during the early 1930's and had been lured to Stowe in 1936 to give ski lessons. Years later, he recalled that, when he arrived in January, 1936, there wasn't a single flake of snow on the ground anywhere in Vermont, and none came down for *another month.* His total gross income that first season was $500!

During the 1930's, the State of Vermont had worked with the Civilian Conservation Corps, a Depression-spawned agency that provided jobs for unemployed young men. A CCC camp had been set up at the base of Mt. Mansfield, and a series of downhill trails had been cleared: trails with old, and (for the most part) now forgotten names, like Chin Clip, Tear Drop, Steeple, Nose Dive, Perry Merrill, and S-53 (the latter taken from the government's designation for the CCC camp. S-53 was widened several years later and became the famous "National" trail).

While Sepp struggled to build up his ski school on the Toll House slope, Lowell Thomas and Roland Palmedo had built the single chair lift in 1941, and Stowe was launched as one of the East's leading ski areas. After World War II, Neil Starr, whose insurance empire included the American Home Insurance Co. (which now insures about three quarters of the ski areas in the country), bought out the Thomas group. He put Sepp in charge of the operation, and a program of expansion followed.

By 1960, Stowe had three chair lifts, two T-Bars, six mountain restaurants, and two hotels. It was a large, well-run operation, with the resources of one of the country's largest companies behind it. Nevertheless, Snyder's visit in 1960 was a disappointment. After skiing all the familiar trails and stopping at the Foster Place to visit old friends, he drove south with the feeling that nothing really was happening there. No new facilities had been built in the last five years;

the trails were narrow and completely ungroomed; and it was bitterly cold. What a difference from southern Vermont, he thought. For all its noisy lifts, Mt. Snow is really the better ski mountain, he concluded—much warmer, and, right now, with better snow.

Mad River Glen, the last stop in the tour, was just what it had always advertised itself to be—"a particular place for particular people." After selling his interest in the Stowe single chair lift to Neil Starr in the late 1940's, Roland Palmedo and some of his friends had come down to Warren and built another lift just like the one at Stowe. This time, Roland had announced, they were going to keep the area small and simple. And small it has remained ever since. The skiing was, and still is, tough and challenging—partly because the terrain is steep and partly because it is so ledgy. Wherever there's a ledge, there will also be blue ice. Mad River was famous for its ice in 1960, but the Mad Riverites didn't care. That made it even more challenging and kept the snow bunnies away. It surely was a particular place!

By March, Snyder had completed his survey of Vermont's six major areas. Each had a distinct flavor, which, for the most part, reflected the personality of the founder, and, consequently, each was completely different from its neighbor.

It had been an interesting tour; but, with a confidence born mostly of ignorance, Snyder felt that he and his associates should be able to design and build a resort on Stratton that would knock the spots out of this competition.

Design of a Ski Area

Between the field trips, design work continued on Stratton. To be certain they were getting the best advice on trail layout and base area design, they hired Sel Hannah of Franconia as a consultant.

Sel is another of the pioneers who has had a major hand in creating the resorts we take so much for granted today. Sadly, most of these rugged individuals are unknown or forgotten today or, like Fred Pabst, have passed from the scene. Sel was a member of our 1936 Olympic Ski Team, and so was a teammate of three other skiing greats: Dick Durrance, Steve Bradley and Ted Hunter.

After the 1936 Olympics, Sel settled down to potato farming in his native New Hampshire. Finding himself increasingly called upon for advice on trail layout and design, he organized a little consulting firm which he called "Snow Engineering Company." It was this firm that Snyder and Smith called in for advice.

In 1960, there was only one way to decide where to build lifts and trails. The designer climbed the mountain on foot. He had no detailed contour maps to help him—only his eye and his experience as a skier guided him. He looked for ledges and springs; he tried to take advantage of the terrain and to estimate what effect the wind would have, once the trees were cut. After examining the ground in the summer, he would return in the winter and ski the mountain. This took great skill and was dangerous, because there was no way of telling whether or not a fallen tree might be lurking just under the surface of the snow.

After weeks of this "cruising," as it was called, he would settle on locations for his lifts and liftlines. These he would "center-line" by fastening strips of colored plastic tape to trees at intervals of 25 ft. or so. Next came the trails, and these were even more difficult. Much is written about golf-course design and the skills of Robert Trent Jones, but laying out a golf course is relatively simple compared to the trail system of a major ski area. A single Stratton Mountain ski trail is as long from summit to base as the distance spanning nine golf holes. It covers terrain far steeper and rockier. Once cut, bulldozed, and seeded, it can be altered but little, whereas most golf course holes are modified pretty much at will. When Stratton first opened in 1961, seven miles of trails had been completed, the equivalent of two golf courses. By 1981, this had been expanded to 56 miles, the equivalent of 18 golf courses.

Before Sel Hannah arrived in early March, 1960, Bob Wright had already located the base and summit lift terminals and had center-lined three lift lines. Now, the two men put on their skis at Taylor Hill Road and climbed until they reached a small glacial terminal moraine at an elevation of 2,100 ft. There, Wright had found a wide flat area that could be used for parking. From here, it was about 7,500 feet to the north summit—too far for one chair-lift. So, he proposed to build two lifts in tandem, one to be 3,000 ft. up from this proposed based, and the other 4,500 ft. long. There was a knoll about 3,000 ft. up from this proposed base, and this, Wright felt, would be an ideal mid-station.

After two days of scouting, Sel reported to Snyder and Smith:

"Most of the time when I'm hired by people to advise on building a ski area, I tell them to forget it, usually because the mountain isn't any good. But I'm not going to discourage you fellows. You have an ideal ski mountain here."

He went on to explain that he looked at five factors in evaluating prospects: (1) vertical rise—that is, the difference in elevation from summit to base; (2) average snowfall over the winter; (3) width of terrain—i.e., how long is the summit and how wide the base?; (4) how smooth and developable is the terrain? A ledgy mountain is going to be much more expensive to build on and will have more ice; and, finally (5) how close is the area to major population centers?

Stratton Mountain was outstanding in every one of these categories, he concluded. It appeared to him that there was about as much vertical rise as for any eastern ski area. The Weather Bureau figures showed an average of 180 inches of snow. The width of terrain was phenomenal; the summit was nearly a mile long and skiable along its entire length. When fully developed, Stratton should have more skiing than any mountain in the East, he claimed. There were very few ledges, although he felt they should check this after the snow had gone. As far as proximity to population centers, that was pretty obvious—the mountain was within five hours driving time for 35 million people.

He agreed with Wright that the base area should be centered on the terminal moraine. Below that level, the terrain was unsuitable. The flat area that Wright had marked out for parking was perfect, and Bob's initial layout of lift lines and trails also looked good.

For this entire two-day survey and for his resulting opinion, the bill from Hannah was $200, plus expenses!

With all due respect to Hannah's and Wright's expertise, neither Snyder nor Smith was convinced that the base area should be built so far upslope. They preferred a spot down near Orcutt Meadows, which would give them 2,400 ft. of vertical on the northeast face. So, to test this proposition, an expedition of four headed into the woods on March 17—Bob Wright and Frank Snyder on skis, Tink Smith and Elmer Argast (a new member of the team who could supervise construction) on snowshoes.

Once on the terminal moraine, Bob took out his map—an enlargement of the National Survey—to point out his reasons for selecting this location for the base lodge. He was convincing. Snyder recorded the conference with his movie camera. A plastic ribbon was tied to a tree and photographed. On this spot, they all hoped, a big base lodge would be standing the following year.

Therefore, March 17 became the day when it was finally decided to sacrifice several hundred feet of vertical to place the base lodge at 2,100 ft. elevation. Curiously enough, no one questioned the placement of the parking lots. It was the accepted practice in those days to locate them directly alongside the base lodge.

Not until years later did Snyder and Smith realize that the parking lots were in the wrong place. They should have been located so that skiers would first have to walk through a village before reaching the base area. Eventually, they would correct that error; but, for its first two decades, Stratton's base area would look like that of any other day ski area.

Meeting the Challenge of Raising Money

Many evenings were spent that winter in Tink Smith's living room discussing Stratton. One subject they frequently asked themselves: why were they taking on this enormous project? Everyone knew that the ski business was risky. Was there any reason to think that they could run a profitable operation, when Stowe, Sugarbush, and Bromley all seemed to be just barely breaking even?

Frank Snyder felt that they ought to be able to run a more efficient operation and that it could be profitable. Tink Smith's view was different. The project *would* make money for him and his family, he was convinced, and it would provide many jobs for the local residents. He had never been in doubt about that and never would be.

Snyder, Janeway, and Crispe were under no illusions that it would be anything but a dreadful struggle all the way, but if they could succeed in building something great when every present indication made the chances look almost impossible, then success would be twice as sweet—this was the challenge they found irresistible.

But, by March 1960, Snyder was ready to admit that his efforts in New York had failed. Copies of the memorandum had been taken to just about every Wall Street underwriting firm, without a single success. The reaction tended to be offhand—even contemptuous as if they were saying, "Don't bother us; the ski area business is too risky; so please get lost."[4]

To cap it all, neither he nor anyone else had been able to come up with a single private investor. Only two good things had come out of all this activity.

First, Snyder had enlisted the aid and support of Wilkie Bushby. Wilkie was a senior partner at Dewey, Ballantine, Bushby, Palmer & Wood, a large and well-known law firm. Frank had shown him a copy of the memorandum, and his response had been encouraging:

"Don't wait too long to build it, Frank—Laura and I have only a very few years left to ski!"

Over the next ten years, Wilkie's support and advice would be invaluable.

[4] By coincidence, Jack Tweedy, a Denver attorney, and Peter Seibert, a dedicated skier from the World War II Tenth Mountain Division, who were the two major promoters of Vail, Colorado, were attempting the same thing and were equally unsuccessful. The two promoting groups exchanged information and formed friendships that are still strong today. Vail was to open in November, 1962, one year after Stratton.

The second benefit came from an unexpected source and almost by chance. On one of their unsuccessful forays to Wall Street, Vail promoters Jack Tweedy and Peter Seibert had had lunch with Snyder. In the course of a conversation which quite naturally involved a certain amount of comparison of fund raising methods, Tweedy described the deal that he was setting up. Vail Associates had purchased two extensive ranches in the valley. Investors in the limited partnership would receive free skiing passes for life and one or more building sites in the future village.

Snyder carried the idea back to Vermont and talked it over with his associates. Everyone agreed that this might work, but there was a problem: International Paper Company owned all of the base area land and was historically opposed to selling good forest holdings.

Smith brought the problem up with Larry Kugelman, who was the manager of Timberlands for International Paper. Larry was sympathetic. He had known the Smiths for many years—Tink and Dick had been selectively cutting much of IP's acreage on Stratton for all of that time, taking only the mature hardwoods for their wood products business. It had always been a fine relationship, where the big company's timber holdings were carefully harvested for mutual benefit. Larry wasn't opposed to a ski resort on Stratton Mountain or to deeding land on the mountain to Tink, since his company's policy had always been to promote what was called "multiple use" of its forests. (IP had been printing and distributing a sportsmen's map of the area.) But he also had a responsibility to acquire additional timber lands, or, at least, not to lose acreage. Therefore, he was agreeable to a swap—but not to a sale—of land. Larry was a tough trader, and, in the end, Tink had to exchange about five acres of good forest land for every acre of Stratton Mountain base area.

As soon as the IP deal had reached an agreement in principle, Snyder sat down with Wilkie Bushby's lawyers to draw up a pre-incorporation agreement for the new company, which would be named "The Stratton Corporation." After much thought and many conferences, it was decided that stock would be sold in 1,000 share units at $5.00 per share. The purchaser of one unit would be entitled to a lifetime ski pass; the purchaser of two units would receive two lifetime passes, plus free passes for his children until their 21st birthday, plus an option for one acre of private chalet land for $500. It was hoped that 50,000 shares could be sold for a total of $250,000 cash.

A total of 60,000 shares would be issued to Tink Smith, to his brother, Dick, and to Snyder for their land, which was being appraised.

Bank financing was now arranged through an old friend, Joe Adams of Dorset. Joe ran a small plant which turned out wooden bowls and plates. On the side, he was a business finder for the National Commercial Bank of Albany. Through his recommendation, National Commercial's President, Frank McCabe, visited Stratton on May 21 and was sufficiently impressed to make a commitment to loan the new company one dollar for every dollar of equity raised. With this promise, the partners now felt they would have enough money to begin work on the Mountain during the coming summer.

Architecture: Stratton's Alpine Spirit

As the snow melted in the spring, they began to make construction preparations. Tink Smith was going to oversee the job, and he couldn't wait to swing into action.

The first thing that had to be done was to build a work road up to the proposed base area. They planned to start cutting into the woods on Taylor Hill Road, not far from Malvine Cole's house. In all, the road would be two miles long.

Now came the first big purchase—a new TD-15 bulldozer manufactured by International Harvester. Craig Swart was the salesman. Years later, when he was Manager of Stratton's Real Estate Department, he would laugh about that sale. The price was $25,000, on a lease purchase agreement, and he was afraid that he would not be paid.

Tink Smith had been busy lining up good men to do the clearing and bulldozing, and he was finding

Frank Snyder atop the new TD-15.

some of the best: Wally Roberts, Lester Williams, Paul Brazer, and Ray Brooks. They became the nucleus of that important group called the "mountain men."

Meanwhile, design had to begin on a base lodge. They had already selected Alexander "Sandy" McIlvaine. One of the old Foster Place regulars, Sandy was a distinguished architect who had done the base lodge/hotel at Squaw Valley, as well as many ski chalets across the country. He liked to tell friends that one of his first jobs had been to assist in the re-design and reconstruction of the White House in the 1940's. When President Truman wanted to build a second-story balcony under the famous portico of the White House, all of Washington was shocked. The firm McIlvaine was then working for designed it, and President Truman was delighted. Later, when daughter Margaret's piano fell through the floor, it became obvious that the White House needed extensive repairs. McIlvaine did much of the work.

Snyder wanted a base lodge that had something of an alpine appearance. It had to seat at least 500 people and should be easily expandable. McIlvaine was somewhat disturbed at these specifications. He didn't think Austrian architecture suited a New England resort, and he didn't see why such a large building was necessary. He was most reluctant to go ahead on these terms. On the other hand, he was enthusiastic about the Stratton Mountain project and had tried to help find investors over the last four months. He was curious about the new financing plans.

"I don't think it'll work," he said. "There is only one way a ski area can be financed. It has to have an angel. Stowe had its angel in Neil Starr; Walter Paepke was Aspen's angel, and Alec Cushing was Squaw Valley's. You are going to be Stratton's."

Frank said, "Absolutely not. My plan is to help get it started with Tink Smith and the others and to leave management to a staff in Vermont."

"Well, lots of luck. I think you're going to find that you'll be signing all the checks."

McIlvaine did agree with Frank that a more sophisticated ski area design was going to have to be made; along with a new approach to investors. He liked the idea of the free ski passes and land options, plus a vigorous program of cocktail and dinner parties at which a model, brochures, and a movie would be presented. He promised to do what he could to find people who seemed interested.

This was the sales method the corporation eventually used successfully, not only to bring in stockholders over the rest of 1960, but also for selling debentures in 1961 and 1962.

Later in the Spring, Snyder decided to combine a Moore & Munger business trip with a visit to Austria in the hope of producing some good ideas for architecture. He contacted the Austrian State Travel Bureau, explaining that he wanted to see buildings that were constructed of wood. There were only two places in Austria, he was told, where mountain buildings of this kind existed. One was the village of Alpach; and the other was the Wildschonau Valley. The Bureau prepared an itinerary and made reservations. On May 6, the Snyders drove into the beautiful village of Alpbach, 50 kilometers east of Innsbruck.

The twentieth century seemed to have passed by Alpbach. There were no ski lifts, no skiers, and only two hotels. In the center of the village was an old place identified with faded paint as the "Jakober Haus, 1642." As soon as he laid eyes on it, Snyder decided that this could be the model.

The house was half timbered, with the entrance in the center of one gable end and two windows evenly spaced on either side of the door. A balcony completely surrounded the second floor, with a second small balcony extending out from the third floor. Snyder photographed it from every angle, with the occupants curiously observing him. The resulting pictures were used by McIlvaine to design the facade of Stratton's base lodge.

Construction of the Ski Area Begins

June 11 was the red-banner day when work on the mountain was officially to begin. Craig Swart had delivered the TD-15 bulldozer to the Day Farm on Taylor Hill Road, and everyone in the promoting group assembled to watch it being unloaded from its flatbed trailer. Tink Smith had ordered a special feature for the dozer, something called a "Drott Four-in-One Bucket Loader." The blade was shaped like a large scoop and could open and close in such a way that it could pick up and move very large objects. His plan was to use this for grubbing and moving tree stumps.

The driver was Wally Roberts. With movie cameras whirring, Wally climbed into the machine and clanked down the road a quarter of a mile to the spot where the work road was to start. Again, it was all done just for show, because the real work would not start until Monday, June 13.

Four men showed up to start work that morning. The chain saws revved up and trees began to topple. To an outsider, it probably looked as if they were just cutting another logging road, and, in fact, that is how IP officially regarded it for the next few months—until the formal lease could be signed. Trees were dropped, and the trunks laid alongside the right-of-way for neighbors to cut up and carry away. Out ahead of everybody was Tink Smith, "eye-balling" the route.

A month later, they had almost reached what was to be the base area. By now, a second big bulldozer had been purchased, an HD-16 made by Allis-Chalmers. It was a monster, bigger than the first one. Lester Williams was assigned as operator, and progress towards the future base area accelerated.

Meanwhile, the corporation had moved into the Day farmhouse on Taylor Hill Road and had converted it into an office. Another key person now joined the team. This was Irene Benson, a marvelous and diminutive business lady who had handled Ed Janeway's bookkeeping for years. She came over to the new office to perform the same function on the Stratton books. Before long, she was a full-time employee and, for the next seven years, she actually ran the Stratton Corporation office, drawing up deeds and contracts, handling personnel problems, and, in many ways, really running the Company.

By August 6, they had cleared the road and upper parking lot and were just starting in the base area. Smith, Janeway, and Snyder stood on the knoll where the base lodge was going to be built. Enough of the area had been cleared so that they could see the summit a mile and a half away. At that moment, Wally Roberts climbed down from his bulldozer and walked over to the group. Smith pointed up towards the summit and said,

"Wally, you're going right up to there."

Wally looked toward the summit for a moment, scratched his head and said,

"By Gawd, I hope not."

But, by God, he did!

They were starting up the first lift line—what is now called the Suntanner. Months earlier, Bob Wright had center-lined it, along with the two other lift lines scheduled for clearing—what would later be named the Tyrolienne and North American. But Wright's departure had left them without a full time expert who understood trail design and who could make the decisions on how wide to cut, and more important, where to leave trees uncut.

They brought the problem to Sel Hannah. Sel knew just the man—Gene Gillis—who had been working for Snow Engineering, overseeing some lift construction in Canada. He had free time and could come down to Stratton right away.

Gene was a native of Bend, Oregon. He had been on the 1948 U.S. Olympic Ski Team, but had been badly injured racing for the Harriman Cup at Sun Valley that year and so had to retire from racing.

He had then decided to make a career in the ski business by learning all he could about the design and construction of lifts and trails. By the time he arrived at Stratton, he had helped build several ski resorts and had supervised the construction of eight chair lifts.

Skiing comes to the mountain: Stratton's first trails, designed by Gene Gillis.

Tall, blonde, and handsome, Gene made an instant hit. He knew his business, worked hard, and was remarkably quiet. It's hard to say which of these characteristics was more respected by the mountain men. His manner reminded many people of Gary Cooper—he had an "aw shucks" modesty that was disarming and accomplished more than he would have with any hard-fisted bossing.

Gene's first job was to "string" the sides of the lift lines. This is standard practice. Starting at the top, the designer slowly walks down through the woods, unrolling orange plastic tape and securing it to trees and bushes. The line marks the edge of the area to be cleared—everything on one side is cut; everything on the other is left untouched. It sound simple, but isn't. Good trees must be saved, whenever possible. Brooks and wet areas have to be avoided. Aesthetics enter into it, too. A straight line is unattractive, and so must always be scalloped.

Within a few days, Gene had finished stringing what was to become Suntanner and Tyrolienne. Both were to be wider at the bottom than the top—one of Gene's trademarks, which he carried out even more carefully on the upper mountain.

After finishing Suntanner and Tyrolienne, he climbed to the summit. Disliking the location of the upper lift line, he moved it to the left, so as to gain wind protection from a gentle ridge, and then center-lined and strung it. This trail is now called the North American.

Over the next four months, Gene laid out every trail that was to be completed for the opening: North American, Tamarack, Rime Line, Suntanner, Tink's

Link, Old Smoothie, Ethan's Alley, Mitten, Wanderer (later renamed Beeline) and Spillway Glade (later renamed Yodeler). Before he left Stratton seven years later to return to his native West, Gene had designed and built every trail on the northeast flank of the mountain, with the exception of Polar Bear and Grizzly Bear.

On July 22, the meeting of the Incorporators of the Stratton Corporation took place in Luke Crispe's office in Brattleboro. Directors elected were: Elmer Argast, Luke Crispe, Ed Janeway, Tink Smith, Dick Smith, and Frank Snyder. The first meeting of the Board took place a few minutes later. By the flip of a coin, Smith was elected Chairman, and Snyder President. Bob Wright was elected Vice President in Charge of Ski Operations, and Elmer Argast Comptroller. Resolutions were passed setting up National Commercial Bank as transfer agent and registrar, and authorizing NCB to issue stock upon execution of the pre-incorporation agreements by investors. Smith and Snyder were instructed to draw up formal leases with International and St. Regis Paper Companies.

The second meeting of the Board was held a week later on Friday, July 29. Pre-incorporation agreements had been signed by all members of the promoting group, with the exception of Malvine Cole, Bob Wright, and Grant Hubley. Unless they signed by July 31, the shares offered to them under the agreement would lapse. Malvine arrived at the meeting and was prevailed upon to sign up, whereupon she was issued 500 shares of stock.

A long discussion was now held with Bob Wright. He simply refused to sign. So it was that, the person who, more than anyone else, had launched the Stratton Mountain Ski Area, irrevocably broke his connection with it.

Financing Stratton with Stock

On August 24, stock was issued to the first 21 limited equity shareholders—42,000 shares for a total of $210,000 cash.[5] Three weeks later, the Board signed a contract with Gerald E. Morrissey, Inc. of Bennington to build the base lodge shell at a price of $77,162. Contracts were also executed with Snow Engineering for trail design and lift specifications, and with Allen & Company of Bennington for a master land plan. A draft of the formal lease with International Paper was also approved.

Morrisey's men were on the job within days. When excavation for the base lodge commenced in September, everyone received a pleasant surprise. It had been assumed that they would have to do extensive blasting. Instead, the back hoe came up with pure, yellow beach sand!

By mid-October, the concrete walls were rising above grade. A barbecue was held for the local people on Saturday, the 16th. It was a foggy, rainy day, but 88 people showed up, and the rain held off, helping to make the affair a success. The *Brattleboro Reformer* had a newspaperman present, and this article appeared in the paper the next day:

> STRATTON—Big business is coming to Stratton—to Winhall too—but the less than 300 persons who make up the two small towns are viewing the future "boom" with reserved optimism.
>
> The new Stratton Corp., headed by a Connecticut man, is gouging the north side of the isolated peak that lies in both towns and constructing a Swiss chalet-type lodge for a major ski development which aims at an eventual 20 trails, a 28-acre lake for boating, swimming, and fishing, and an 18-hole championship golf course.
>
> But it is with a provisional sort of reserved optimism that many people among Stratton's 27-odd population are looking forward to the "new industry." The attitude is much the same with Winhall's 245 citizens.
>
> "We think it's good. Most people do," said a Stratton housewife, surveying the muddy area where the selectmen of the two towns were chatting with the developers. "Not everyone is so sure," she added, "but time will tell."
>
> "It will probably bring more business around here—lodging places, eating facilities, and employment for some of the men," said a quiet man standing apart from the barbecue crowd.
>
> "We see a bright future," said a woman seated at an improvised barbecue table, "but there is some question of what kind of people will be coming in—the recreation trade, I mean."

Recalling those busy days in a *Stratton Magazine* article, Irene Benson wrote:

> "We opened an office in the old Day house on Taylor Hill Road that Frank had bought

[5] Their names:

Elizabeth W. Allen	C. Winthrop Hoyt
Philip K. Allen	Edward G. Janeway
John Barry	Elinor W. Janeway
Mrs. Stephen Bresko	John A. Lautz
Wilkie Bushby	John O. Morris
Roy B. Chapin	Dr. Pinckney Phyfe
A. Luke Crispe	Virginia F. Scudder
Dr. W. O. Fillebrown	Jessie P. Snyder
George B. Gibbons, Jr.	Edward P. Snyder, Jr.
Dr. George T. Gildea	William Taylor
G. E. Herre	A. Lindsey Thompson
Willard A. Kiggins, Jr.	

as one of the preliminaries of acquiring enough property to carry out the burgeoning plans. (The Day house later became the Arnold Palmer Golf Academy.) There was a desk, one four-drawer filing cabinet and the coffee pot which brewed from the time I got there in the morning until I left—not only for Elmer Argast and myself but also for the crew who wandered in and out.

"It was October, 1960, and getting cooler. Each day when I came to work, I built a wood fire in the old kitchen stove which quickly warmed the room. I heard the cutting and burning up in the "base area" and the big machines moving the soil around to create a building site for the lodge and parking lots, but somehow there wasn't time to go see.... Fires burned day and night as everyone hurried to get everything done before the snow came. As it turned out, everyone worked through the winter anyway."

On November 4, the *Brattleboro Reformer* covered the mountain again:

"STRATTON—The clearing and grading operation on Stratton Mountain is racing towards completion, ahead of schedule, according to a report issued here today by Elmer Argast, Director and Manager of the Stratton Corp. Argast attributed the achievement to an ambitious work force of 16 men on a six-day, rain or shine program and "the greatest concentration of machines at a private project in northern New England."

" 'Outside of highways and federal dams,' said Argast, 'I know of no other regional development in progress with a larger assemblage of earth-moving equipment than we have here on Stratton. What would have taken a generation in times past, we are doing in a matter of months.'

"Since late June, Argast's report showed the Stratton Corp. has constructed a two-mile road over six streams and cleared, graded and readied for seeding more than two miles of lift lines and ski trails, crossed by 12 streams. The Corporation's men and machines, he said, are working against the coming of deep snow to get as much done as possible this year, with plans to resume next June."

By December, the limited equity offering was closed out as planned at $300,000. A total of 18,000 shares were sold to 11 investors during the last three months of the year, bringing in $90,000 cash, and another 5,000 shares were issued for past services or to settle promoters' claims against the company.[6]

At the year's end, there were 39 stockholders: 32 had contributed $300,000 in cash; three (Smith, Smith's brother Dick, and Snyder) had contributed approximately 1,000 acres of land; and four had contributed services. Bob Wright had brought suit against the company and had settled for a cash payment of $12,500.

A marathon directors meeting was held on December 30, in which a myriad of details were finalized relating to stock issuance, settlement of claims, and other financial matters. Three vital subjects were under consideration at that meeting:

First, Sel Hannah and Gene Gillis had drawn up detailed specifications against which lift manufacturers were expected to bid. This was something new in the ski business. Ski areas had always accepted the manufacturer's specifications in the past. Now, some manufacturers seemed to be having difficulty in adjusting to Stratton's requirements. Two of them, Riblet and De Savio, simply disregarded Stratton's specifications and bid on their own. As a result, their bids were discarded. In all, 17 manufacturers bid, and a decision would have to be made soon.

The second matter was further financing. A preliminary prospectus was presented to the Board. It offered 650, $1,000 debentures, maturing in 1981. Lift privileges would go along with them: one privilege for one bond; family privileges for three bonds. The plan was to file with SEC early in the new year. As it turned out, the issue was not filed until late spring and did not clear SEC until September, a delay that threw the financial planning into serious disarray.

Finally, there was the matter of an access road. The *Brattleboro Reformer* had written an article about it on December 6:

"Over at Stratton, there will be no skiing this winter, but the progress is no less impressive. This is a much larger undertaking than is generally realized—and you have to see it to appreciate it.... The big problem yet to be solved at Stratton Mountain Ski Development is just how the heck the area will be served by at least one good access road. The approach will have to be a lot better than it is now, in order to attract and handle the traffic the investment will need in order to justify itself—and in order for the surrounding area

[6] Those who purchased stock during the last quarter of 1960 were:

Dr. David Babbott
Emil A. & David Petke
Dr. N. W. Wawro
Dr. David Wasley
Arthur B. Hamm
Robert E. Pluff
Howard F. Whitney
F. Ellsworth Jannicky
Kenneth Ives, Jr.
Douglass Mabee
B. Allen Rowland

Those who received stock for services:

Elmer Argast
Malvine Cole
Grant Hubley
Alexander McIlvaine

> to get the economic benefit it should get with such an impressive ski area in its midst. The Stratton development deserves exactly as good a deal from the State of Vermont and the surrounding area as was obtained for Sugarbush and Killington."

Ed Janeway had spoken to the new Governor, Ray Keyser, and also to the people in the Highway Department. He felt there was strong support for the road, but, of course, a special bill had to pass in the current legislature, which was scheduled to meet in mid-January. In an ordinary year, such a bill would have no serious obstacles, but 1961 was no ordinary year in Vermont politics. Many worthwhile projects, including Stratton's, were to be bottled up in Committee for the next seven months, while the Governor and Senator Ace Bloomer of Rutland fought it out for control of the State.

Finding the Best People

Nineteen sixty-one was a heavy snow year. There were five storms in January, which piled up the snow so deep on Stratton that all work was halted and the machines laid up. For a few weeks, stillness descended on the mountain. It was the peace before the storm.

Irene Benson recalled:

> "We moved the office to the Lincoln Maples (now known as Haig's), which was a lovely old inn in Bondville that the company now owned. We added another file. Regular weekend Board meetings developed, and it was always a Saturday meeting that grew into two days, as the work load accumulated. I made sandwiches for the lunch on these days, so that no time would be lost, and the coffee pot was exchanged for a larger one."

Even though the scheduled opening was 11 months away, so much had to be done. Water supply and sewage disposal systems had to be designed and built. A plan of development of lots had to be completed, and secondary roads laid out and built. The interior of the base lodge had to be designed and built. Charles "Bud" Lench, of Lench Associates, was brought into the picture. His help and expertise were invaluable. Personnel had to be found to head up the various departments: ski school, ski patrol, restaurant, ski shop, and cashier. Chair lifts had to be selected and ordered, and, most of all, the money situation had to be monitored. Events were beginning to overtake the little hard-working Board, and they knew it.

At least, the chair lifts were in good hands. Gene Gillis and Elmer Argast had put together a spread sheet, with some 30 critical requirements down the side and with the manufacturers' names across the top. After much study, they decided to recommend the manufacturer who had sent in the highest bid, Robert Heron of Denver, Colorado. For three double chair lifts, he had quoted $450,000 delivered to Stratton. Gillis estimated that construction cost would be $150,000.

Gillis solved another problem, when, on April 8, he introduced to the Board the man who was to make his name almost synonymous with Stratton Mountain.

Before Emo Henrich strode into the Lincoln Maples sitting room that was used for Board meetings, Gene had already filled in the directors on his background: born and raised in Innsbruck, he had attended a university and had a degree in electrical engineering. Skiing was his first love, however, and he had obtained his Austrian ski instructor certification—a two-year effort that carries great prestige in the United States as well as Austria. He had then invented a new type of ski for summer glacier skiing, which he called "ferngleiters," and which are now very popular in the Alps. He had come to the United States as a racing coach at Sugar Bowl Ski Area in the Sierras. At present, he was assistant director of the ski school there and at Othmar Schneider's ski school at Portillo, Chile.

Gillis had met Emo at Sugar Bowl and had been enormously impressed—not only with his skiing ability, which was top notch (Emo had won the famous Silver Belt race there in his first year), but also with the way he handled people.

In the conversation that followed, Emo said that he hoped to operate an Austrian ski school, teaching the technique that was just then being perfected by Professor Kruckenhauser at the Austrian State School of Ski Instruction. He also proposed that music be made a large part of the ski school function. He wanted to hire a number of Austrian instructors who also had musical ability and to build up a little band. The minutes of that meeting record the interview:

> "Mr. Henrich was interviewed at great length by the Board of Directors and the general plans of the ski school were discussed with him and Mr. Gillis. Mr. Gillis highly recommended the employment of Mr. Henrich. Mr. Janeway then moved the following motion:
>
> "That the Corporation employ Emo Henrich as Assistant Ski School Director at a salary of $4,500 for the period beginning December 15, 1961 and ending April 15, 1962 and that the Corporation furnish, free of rent to Mr. Henrich, an apartment or similar accommodations for himself, wife and child."

Stratton Mountain Ski School

In April, 1961, when Emo Henrich came to Bondville to be interviewed for the position of Stratton Ski School Director, he laid out his ideas of how a ski school should fit into a winter resort's operations.

First of all, he said the primary purpose of a ski school is to create new and loyal customers for the resort by concentrating on the novices (both adult and children), bringing them quickly to the point where they can use the lifts and trails safely and begin to *enjoy* the sport. The beginner is the most important customer that the resort has, he emphasized, and so there must be novice lifts and trails for them. He also said there must be a place in the ski school for every age group and every level of skiing ability, so that every member of a family can be taken care of.

Skiing should be fun: Walter Heigl demonstrates the Ski School philosophy.

Secondly, and only a little less important, all the instructors must ski the same way and teach the same way. This means continuous training and drilling of instructors—a discipline that is neglected at most resorts.

But teaching is not where the instructor's responsibility ends, he added. Because he is the only employee that most of the customers meet and get to know, the instructor is the company's ambassador to the public—the salesman. It is, therefore, very important that he convey a good impression of warmth and hospitality by being courteous and helpful. Henrich said that, if hired, he would attempt to create this kind of ski school at Stratton.

There was one further dream he wanted to bring to reality at Stratton and that was a music program. He had always wanted to form a "little band" and to have music and dancing in the base lodge every day.

It was a well thought-out program that he presented that day. He was hired forthwith, and the Stratton Mountain Ski School has followed that original blueprint ever since.

In the first year there were only seven full time instructors: Tony Egger, Ernst Schütz, Walter Heigl,

Dinko Bertoncelj, Adi Scheidle, Hans Klimmer, and Andy Burton. They lived in the old Lincoln Maples Inn which lacked heat upstairs. Schütz was an original Outward Bound type who lived only for his big game hunting in summer (he was reportedly a famous poacher in his native Austria) and absolutely refused to get inside of a car (he clung to the ski rack on top of the ski school jalopy that took them back and forth to the Mountain), and had the misfortune—as he saw it—of having to live next door to Toni Egger. Their rooms were connected by an air register, and Toni was a chain smoker. The smoke drifted into Schütz's room. He complained, opened his window wide, and kept it open. It was then Egger's turn to complain that cold air was coming back through the register and was freezing him. So, he smoked even harder. That argument went on all winter.

Toni Egger lives in his native St. Johann in Tirol, where he still teaches skiing. After leaving Stratton in 1964, Ernst Schütz spent years traversing Montana and Wyoming on foot in winter and summer, hunting for his food with his rifle. Then he went on to Alaska, where it is reported, he became a U.S. Forester, settling down in a cabin with an eskimo lady for a while.

After Stratton opened to the public, Emo Henrich wasted no time getting his music program underway. The carpenters were still trying to finish the Base Lodge when he held his first Tyrolean Evening in what is now the Bear's Den. There was no carpet, and the furniture had to be carried in. Also, as Emo recalls it, there was only one paying customer. Everyone else in the room was an employee.

The word soon went out that these Tyrolean Evenings were fun and, before long, the "Stratton Mountain Boys," as Emo named them, became an institution playing to sell-out crowds in the Base Lodge.

As the school expanded, Henrich divided it into sections, each with its own supervisor. From opening day onward until near the end of the 1980–1981 season, Associate Director Hans Palmer conducted the Ski Desk in the Base Lodge, dispensing tickets, making announcements in four languages, and calming upset parents. Herman Herzog was Assistant Director out on the slopes. A consummate technician, Herzog drilled new instructors until they skiied to his satisfaction and the Ski School soon took on a polished and disciplined appearance. Also created in the first year was the "Big Cub" school under Ruthie Rowley, who has run it capably ever since. Two years later the same idea for the very little ones was put to reality and the "Little Cub Ski School" was founded under Muriel Bouton's fine supervision.

Then, Adi (The Great) Gruber came over from his native Innsbruck to become bandleader of the Stratton Mountain Boys, a job he did with great skill and devotion for over a decade. In this, he was ably assisted by Hans Kremser, Otto Egger, Toni Lechner and, in more recent years—Kasi Lindlbauer and Stefan Schernthaner, who is now bandleader of this nationally known and very successful group of musical ski instructors.

It is impossible, unfortunately, to give credit to all the fine young men and women who have contributed to the Ski School and its "little band" of Stratton Mountain Boys over the years, but mention should be made of Stratton's professional racers. When the original pro racing association—IPSRA—collapsed in 1964, The Stratton Corp. joined with several other resorts to keep the idea alive and hired several of the racers themselves to teach at Stratton when they were not on the road racing. Ernst Hinterseer, 1960 Olympic Gold Medal winner, and Hias Leitner, Silver Medalist, became Stratton employees for the next few years, pretty well cleaning up on the pro circuit and bringing Stratton's name far and wide, while at the same time adding a big lift to the Ski School.

Later, Herman Goellner joined the group—first as a racer, then as a free style champion, and finally as racing coach. Goellner's skill, self-discipline, and devotion to clean living and sportsmanship have made him an inspiration for a whole generation of young ski racers.

Succeeding Herman in free style, Stefan Schernthaner became Eastern Champion of Free Style Skiing and the head of the free style movement in our Ski School. Today, the Ski School carries on with the same methods and objectives of two decades ago, although many of the faces have changed. Hans Palmer has retired. Herman Herzog is a banker in his native Maria Alm, where his brother, Adi, still teaches skiing. "Fat" Toni Lechner is just a little bit fatter. He owns and operates the Hotel Sonnberg above Zell am See and tends his own bar. Walter Heigl has his own pension in Igls, and Adi Gruber has built "Haus Stratton" in Axams, near Innsbruck. Adi Scheidle, Dinko Bertoncelji, Werner Pflaum, and Gerhard Wildauer have ski schools of their own.

The Stratton Mountain Boys seem to get better every year. Their popularity has certainly soared. They are now booked months in advance and travel all over the United States, bringing the name of Stratton far and wide. They have cut their third record, and it is selling even faster than the others did. They continue to bring music, fun, and laughter to thousands, just as Emo Henrich had envisioned that day in April, 1961.

Wife and child, of course, were Annedore and their infant daughter, Mercedes, who is known to one and all at Stratton as "Benzi." From the above minutes, it is evident that the corporation's clerk, Luke Crispe, had not yet gotten the right spelling of Emo's first name.

When, years later, Emo was asked by *The Stratton Magazine* why he decided to go to Stratton, he replied:

> "The people at Stratton were committed to building and maintaining a quality resort, which was most important to me. After quality, everything else will fall into place. Anyway, we toured the Mountain, and I could see by the terrain that this would be the perfect place for a ski school. The upper and lower sections gave plenty of area for a novice as well as the expert. I walked up the Mountain, since there were no lifts, and skied down between the stumps."

Next, the Board voted to hire Peter Pappas, co-owner of the Paradise Restaurant in Bennington, to operate the cafeteria and restaurant. The salary was to be $7,500 plus a percentage of the gross over $100,000. On the same day, it was agreed to contract with Charles Sonnenfeld and Peter Pringham of Norse House, an outstanding New York ski shop, to staff and run the rental and repair shop.

The terse wording of the minutes of this meeting give no idea of the effort behind these two decisions. Every step the directors were making was on new ground. Although they were experienced businessmen (and probably no new ski area ever had a more talented and devoted Board to guide it in its early days), they were beginners in the field of ski area management. None of them had ever built a lift, or a water or sewer system; none had run a restaurant or a ski school. So it was vital that they find the best people available to fill these and other departments in the new company. This took much scouting. Gillis had been given the job of searching for a ski school director, Frank Snyder the task of finding a good ski shop franchisee, and Tink Smith the assignment of locating a restaurant manager. So it went—from one project to the next, week after week.

Two decisions were made in May which, although totally dissimilar, had long-reaching effects on the company's future.

The first was the hiring of Aldren Watson to design a logo. Two ideas were suggested by the directors: one was to adopt the snow goose, since the mountain was on the snow goose flyway. The second was to use the black bear, because the Indian name for the mountain had been "Manicknung," meaning "Home of the Bear." Watson prepared several drawings of each, and the Board selected the bear logo.

The second was to retain James Laubach of Brattleboro to monitor the capital expenditures program. Two weeks after having been retained, Laubach reported that the current capital budget of $1,100,000 would be exceeded by something on the order of $300,000 by opening day in December 1961.

Rising Costs Answered with More Stock

It had been the strategy to build the ski area mostly with equity and debenture funds. When the financing plan was adopted back in August 1960, it had been estimated that the total construction cost going into opening would be $900,000, and the decision was to raise $250,000 in cash from a limited equity group plus $650,000 from debenture buyers. In November, the equity group had been expanded to $300,000, as the costs began to go up, but it was decided not to change the debenture offering, since it had been pretty much finalized. By May 1961, the capital estimate was up to $1,100,000. Even by selling out the bond issue during the summer and fall, they expected to have to borrow $150,000.

Laubach's report came as a shocker. Instead of $150,000, now they would have to borrow $450,000. The first thing they did was to drive down to Albany for a conference with Bill Davison, top loan officer for the National Commercial. Laubach went over the numbers for Davison and pointed out that the company might have to borrow considerably more than $450,000, if the bond issue went flat. Davison said he had no problem with this. The bank would back them, he declared, beyond Frank McCabe's commitment of dollar-for-dollar.

Back in Bondville, they restudied their capital plan to see how they might raise more money privately. A long argument ensued that extended over several weeks. It was the opinion of the company's auditor, Roy B. Chapin, that the best way was for the company to issue demand notes to its stockholders for $300,000. Snyder was unwilling to do this, pointing out that this is always the last card that a sinking corporation plays. He much preferred a second round of stock. If successful, it would increase the amount that the company should be able to borrow in case the bond issue were to fall completely on its face.

In the end, he won the argument and, on July 17, the Board voted to offer 94,000 shares to existing stockholders at $3.50 on a ratio of two shares offered for every three shares owned.

A Green Light for the Access Road

On July 19, there was good news from the State Capitol:

> "MONTPELIER (AP)—Stratton Mountain's $290,000 ski access road got the green light in the Senate today.
>
> "The upper chamber endorsed the House-passed resolution, as lawmakers noted there is ample precedent for the State to assist in underwriting ski development projects.
>
> " 'The future of the State lies in recreation,' said Senator John O'Brien, D-Chittenden, who noted local developers had raised 80 percent of the capital needed for the project.
>
> "Senator Noel Viens, D-Grand Isle, remarked that the Highways and Bridges Committee was 'certainly treated royally' by Corporation officials during an inspection of the site.
>
> "He said 'with all the money these people are spending, it is no more than right that we give them a helping hand.'
>
> "Senator James L. Oakes, R-Windham, quoting from a report in ski developments drafted by a New Hampshire agency, said Vermont was outdistancing its neighboring state 'because it is placing a heavy emphasis on governmental assistance to private enterprise.'
>
> "Senator Edward G. Janeway, R-Windham, a director of the Stratton Corp., abstained from voting on the resolution."

On the following day, the *Brattleboro Reformer* reported:

> "The bill was finally forwarded to the Governor providing state funds for the road that will cut a new path through the Green Mountains wilderness, bringing skiers and vacationers close to new slopes and unseen evergreens.
>
> "As already in blueprints, the road will right-angle out of Bondville, waking up that sleepy settlement with visitors leaving Route 30 in the village, to slice southwest into the mountainside, top the Stratton foothills, and climb to the base lodge. The lodge, of Tyrolean proportions, is being completed by the Stratton Corp., now developing 1,000 acres as a ski and recreation world.

Right or wrong (and wrong, it was later to appear) the Board had held back on signing contracts for fabricating the lifts, finishing the base lodge, and installing the water and sewer systems. Now, with the road assured, they rushed to sign up Morrissey for the base lodge, Lupton Steel of Pittsfield for the lifts, and Coffey and Teachout Supply Co., Inc. of Colchester, for the water line contract. It was an all-Vermont team that would be working on the mountain and rushing to finish the job by December.

Work on the Mountain Moves Rapidly

On April 22, Minor McLaughlin was hired as public relations director at a salary of $7,500. "Mitch," as he was known, had had the job at Mt. Snow, where Snyder had met him the previous winter. He came highly recommended by John Hooper, who was a Stratton Corporation Stockholder and editor of the *Brattleboro Reformer.* Mitch did a fine job running the marketing effort on a shoestring budget over the next few years, and he was soon promoted to the position of assistant general manager.

Also joining the Corporation (on April 30) was Karl Bauer. Karl was raised in Garmisch-Partenkirchen, Germany's most famous ski resort, where his father had been a mountain guide and where he had learned mountaineering and ski racing. During World War II, he had fought in the German army, had risen to the rank of Lt. Colonel, and was wounded three times.

Snyder remembers Karl's arrival at Stratton. He was standing on the base lodge balcony, when a burly, square man with a small mustache politely approached him, asking for a job.

"We need someone who knows something about dynamite. Do you?" Snyder asked.

"Oh yah. In the German Army, I was a sapper."

"What was a sapper?"

"Oh, we plew up the pridges."

Karl was promptly hired and placed under Gene Gillis along with Casey Rowley. Casey's job was to cut the trees; Karl's to follow the bulldozers and to groom and seed the trails.

The bulldozer work was a specialty at which the Stratton operators had had no experience. Consequently, the corporation hired Ray Parker. After clearing and burning, the future trails presented an incredibly rocky appearance. There was very little exposed ledge, but boulders were everywhere—some of them 10 feet high and 100 tons in weight. Using DC8's, about the largest bulldozers made by Caterpillar, Parker started at the top. The dozers were placed back to back, with their winches almost touching and their cables linked. The downhill-facing dozer then began pushing rock and soil down the slope, while secured by the upper bulldozer. At the end of his pass, he would crank himself uphill, while the upper bulldozer helped by hauling in on its winch.

It was back-breaking work for the drivers; they earned their pay. Down the slope the giant machines crawled, preceded by a 20 foot high berm of soil, rocks, and stumps. The real art lay in burying those rocks and stumps and leaving a smooth surface that could then be groomed.

After Parker's bulldozers were finished, Karl Bauer's men dragged the slope with a York rake hauled by a Bombardier to remove smaller rocks still on the surface. This was followed by hand raking and removal of stones; then fertilizing and seeding. The seed was a combination recommended by the University of Vermont. Haying was the last step—the scattering of loose hay as a mulch to promote germination.

Work was going ahead rapidly everywhere. The lift foundations were being completed in August—a mighty achievement. Each foundation (there were 66 of them) had to be pinned to the ledge rock of the mountain by driving 8-foot 1½-inch diameter reinforcing rods into holes drilled deep into the rock.

The design called for underground drive terminals at the bottom of each lift. These were to be concrete "pill boxes," 20 feet square and 10 feet deep. The two base area terminals didn't create any problems, because the soil was fairly deep, but the mid-station terminal was located on solid granite. This called for an expert, and, one day in September, a gentleman arrived at the base area with a large black attaché case. He was driven by jeep to the mid-station, holding his case carefully in his lap as they jolted up the rough work road.

The terminal site had already been drilled by Karl Bauer with a grid of some 225 holes, 1½ inches in diameter, down to a depth of 10 feet. Having arrived there, the little man opened up his briefcase, revealing neat rows of bottles, each filled with a pale liquid called nitroglycerine.

As Karl watched over his shoulder, the man began dropping bottles into holes. After about ten had gone in without trouble, one got stuck halfway down. He began poking it with a special rod he carried to ram it through the obstruction. At this point, Karl hurriedly left the scene. As he walked swiftly down Suntanner heading for the base lodge, he expected an explosion any second which would blow up the man along with the ledge.

Nothing happened, and later that day, when the expert was ready, the whole thing was detonated. It was a tremendous explosion. After the dust had settled, a neat, square excavation existed where none had been before. Thousands of sharp little stones—none more than three inches in diameter—were spread around the ground for a radius of 300 feet.

Last-minute Fundraising

On August 29, a stockholder meeting was held that approved the new stock issue. Once again, land options and lift privileges were going with the new offering. The entire issue was sold out. Later, all the stockholders were able to exercise their land options and recover their investments—all, that is, except Tink Smith, his brother Dick, and Frank Snyder. Although they earned options on 19 acres of company land as a result of this offering, they never did exercise them.

On September 15, the bond issue finally cleared SEC, and they were ready to run with another fundraising effort. Snyder had found a friend and supporter in Danforth Miller, Jr. of Hartford, Connecticut. Danny was a skier and was employed by a small underwriting firm in Hartford by the name of Cooley & Company. Cooley agreed to sell the issue on a "best efforts" basis.

Danny presented a marketing plan to the Board on September 16. While it was expected that many bonds would be sold at the Stratton office during the season, it was hoped that Danny's effort downcountry would bring in the first $100,000 within 30 days. The SEC approval would be void if this was not accomplished. He set to work with the enthusiastic help of Mrs. Charles Lord, whose energy and contacts helped to bring in many Hartford investors.

But, as the 30 days were about to expire, it became evident that they were not going to make it. Less than 50 bonds had been sold. At this point, Snyder's brother, Phil, stepped into the picture and asked their mother to purchase 100 bonds to save the issue. This Mrs. Snyder did, to the consternation of her investment advisors at Morgan Guaranty Trust Company.

An Industry "First:" Airlifting Lift Towers

October arrived with no lifts, and the word was out that Stratton wasn't going to make it to the opening. The access road right-of-way had barely been cleared, and heavy grading had just begun. The route was fairly gentle. They were lucky in not having much blasting ahead of them, but it was touch and go whether the road could be finished in time, even though the Vermont Highway Department was confident.

At this point, Snyder got a phone call from Serge Gagarin. Serge was an old Foster Place skier—and one of the very best. He worked for United Aircraft and owned a home in Landgrove.

"I hear you're running behind on your lift construction," he said.

Snyder admitted he didn't know how they were going to do it. The steel was just beginning to arrive and probably wouldn't all be there before the end of October.

"Well, have you ever heard of helicopter airlifting of lift towers?"

"No."

"Neither have I, because it's never been done. But I'm sure it can be."

"You've got to be kidding."

"Not at all. Our choppers have been setting power line towers for years, and they service offshore drilling platforms too."

There was a company called Petroleum Helicopters, Inc., he said, that specialized in this work and that owned several very high-powered machines that could lift 6,000 pounds and hold it in position with accuracy. It happened that Sikorsky had just completed maintenance on one of these. The crew was to pick it up in Stratford, Connecticut, and deliver it to Shreveport, Louisiana, toward the end of the month. Serge was sure they could swing by Stratton and do the job.

The deal was quickly made at a price of $9,500. A trailer-load of drums containing special helicopter fuel was dispatched to the mountain on October 23, and the chopper arrived on Thursday, October 26. It was a huge machine, with a crew of two. One flew it. The other sat in an open hatch on the starboard side, with his feet hanging over the edge. From this position, he could see the situation and, with microphone, coach the pilot. A wire cable under the helicopter secured an electrically operated pelican hook.

On Thursday, the operation began. Public relations man Mitch McLaughlin had talked the "Today Show" people into sending up a photographer. The whole process was to be aired on national television. Gene Gillis had the towers carefully laid out in the parking lot. Sheave trains were not yet bolted to them, even though this would have saved a lot of work later on, because he was afraid they might be damaged if a tower had to be laid down on the ground. This turned out to be a wise decision.

The wind was blowing hard on Thursday, and Owen Guidry, the pilot, was afraid to try to set towers. A few trial flights were made up the mountain to check if there was enough room between the foundations and trees, and that was that for the first day. On Friday and Saturday, all the towers were flown and positioned on their concrete bases.

It was dangerous work. Seven or eight trees along the edge of Suntanner and North American had to be dropped, because they were too close to the tower foundations. One of them was still falling when the chopper arrived to place Tower 3 of the upper lift. At another point, the chopper blade nicked a branch, severing it and sending it whirring out towards the spectators.

After the towers came the sheave trains, followed by all of the terminal steel and hundreds of bags of cement. In all, over 200 tons of material were moved into position in a little over 12 hours. All hands were jubilant. Now, they had a good chance of getting the three lifts into operation by Christmas.

Down at the office, however, matters were not as joyful. The debentures weren't selling at all well; unexpected costs were piling up, particularly in the base lodge construction. Snyder had invited Bill Davison to come over to see the helicopter operation, and, after it was completed, to discuss further bank financing. He had been in constant touch with Davison, feeding him the latest numbers each week, and the bank had volunteered that they were impressed with the way Stratton was handling the situation. On the momentous 28th of October, Davison stated that the bank's loan committee had agreed to increase the commitment of $750,000. There was one hooker, though—the directors would have to sign personally. If Stratton hadn't been a financial strain up to this point, it certainly was from here on.

Ironically, the public's impression was that the Stratton Mountain project was marvelously well-financed and simply rolling in money. From the day it opened, Stratton would be regarded as "Vermont's Class Act," as Bill Berry wrote in an article in the September, 1980, issue of *SKI Magazine.*

Stratton Opens for Business

The mountain crew had two more months to put it all together. The weather was rapidly turning, and it was all "cold-finger" work now. The terminal structures were erected, sheave trains hoisted and secured. Then came the massive cables—three of them—and 300 chairs. It was hard, frigid work.

But they made it—just barely. On December 20, 1961 the two lower lifts were inspected by the Tramway Board and opened to the public three days later. On December 29, the upper lift was put into service. On that day, 3,900 skiers deluged the area, according to the 1962 Annual Report. A Christmas week snowstorm dropped 22 inches, and skiing was excellent.

The Vermont Highway Department had also just made the deadline. The road was open—if it could be called a road. The last blasting was completed early in the morning of December 23, and bulldozers were still moving the debris aside, as the first cars arrived. There was no time to lay down gravel, and it was a rough bumpy ride all the way from Bondville that first winter. But the customers were understanding; there were few complaints. Stratton was in business, if on a somewhat Spartan basis.

Martha Sonnenfeld, a Vermonter who was there, remembers it in these words:

> "Another Vermont ski area had finally struggled into existence, and it had been a tough and tiring job. Stratton was now officially open, even though there were only three lifts, an unfinished access road (that would leave much to be desired until the time when it could be paved), and an impressive base lodge with a lot of finishing touches yet to be done. Also lacking were accommodations for food and lodging; the Stratton Mountain Inn would not be ready until the coming fall. But the quality was there, and other ski areas had opened with much less. What Stratton and its people had accomplished was no small achievement. The Vermonters and the non-Vermonters (to coin a word) had worked hand-in-hand to bring this about and a wonderful camaraderie now existed. It was time to have a small celebration.
>
> "The dignitaries were invited, the speeches scheduled, and the menu planned for the banquet. There would also be a fashion show for the ladies, and later singing and dancing—Austrian style. It was not the intention to have a big splash—rather to have a nice pleasant affair to pay honor to the accomplishments.
>
> "When the time arrived on that cold Saturday in January, the crowd of stockholders, friends and hard working Stratton men and women listened and applauded the kind words of the various speakers: Lowell Thomas, the well-known radio broadcaster; Governor of Vermont F. Ray Keyser, a great ski pioneer; and the late Fred Pabst, who built the neighboring ski resort, Big Bromley, and whose favorite explanation of his occupation was, 'I farm snow!'
>
> "Especially important to many was the pres-

Opening Day Celebration, January 18, 1962; on hand are (from left) John Hooper, ***Brattleboro Reformer;*** *unidentified paper company representative; Mitch McLaughlin; and Governor Ray Keyser.*

Caroline and Dick Smith, among the first stockholders and contributors of land, enjoy Opening Day festivities.

ence of Lawrence Kugelman, the executive from International Paper Company, with whom those critical, and seemingly interminable, negotiations for leasing the upper part of the mountain had taken place. Happily it resulted in an agreement that was one of the main steps in making Stratton a possibility.

"It is fitting that mention also be made of a long-time member of the original Stratton staff, Hans Palmer, who manned the ski desk and the base lodge intercom from the very beginning. On that dedication day, Hans did his valiant best to make sure important announcements were clearly and distinctly heard by all. That included some announcements of lesser importance such as, 'Please, Mrs. Bishop, will you be so kind as to get your poodle off the ski slopes? Thank you.' (All of this in Hans' wonderful Viennese accent.) From that time on everyone has been impressed with Hans Palmer's amazing talent for knowing what dog belonged to what owner!

"Even with the distraction of an occasional dog on the slopes, lost car keys, and sometimes—as we have learned—misplaced automobiles, it was all great fun. No one knew for sure the kind of future that awaited a ski area like Stratton, but everyone present that day knew it was bound to make a major bid for Vermont's winter tourist trade."

At the reception following the Saturday banquet, Sally Pabst marveled that "so many skiers would drive up that long dirt road." Snyder agreed. It was a terrible road, bumpy and rutty all the way, but lots of cars were driving up it, and customers were happy—probably because there wasn't any skiing experience in Vermont (or perhaps in all the East) to match it.

And yet, riding the lift one day, Snyder was nonplussed when he asked a young man riding next to him what he thought of Stratton and was told,

"It's a good beginning, but they have a long way to go."

"In what ways?"

"Well, the whole place looks unfinished. They need more trails and lifts, more buildings, more everything."

The young man was right, and his comments were more than a little sobering. Stratton did have a long way to go. Skiers would endure long drives over icy and rutty roads to reach good skiing, and they would put up with bad weather and long lift lines, as long as they could see an effort being made to improve and expand from one year to the next.

For the staff, it was a season of learning-how and making-do. Emo Henrich recalled that first season in an interview for the *Stratton Magazine:*

> "When I began, I had only seven instructors. All of our equipment was in a box chained to a tree where the ski school now stands. It wasn't until the second year that we had an office. They gave me an office in what is now Hubert Schriebl's darkroom. The only entrance was through the men's bathroom. When I hired Peter Cornell, I told him to come with me to the office. When I walked into the bathroom, he stopped; and I had to come back out and get him."

Two of those seven instructors, Adi Scheidle and Dinko Bertoncel, are now ski school directors. Three others—Toni Egger, Adi Gruber, and Walter Heigl—now have their own guest houses in Austria.

All other departments were struggling too. Casey Rowley's four ski patrolmen had no on-the-mountain patrol houses; the maintenance building was a tar paper shack; Peter Pappas didn't have enough working room in the kitchen; and Charley Sonnenfeld had no place to store clothes and ski equipment for Norse House.

But they had opened, and they were running and making an impact on the skiing world. Their financial backs were against the wall, but they had survived up to this point and were confident that they could carry on.

In March, the access road began to collapse. The upper end (above Taylor Hill Road) became impassable during the week of March 23. Cars were detoured left on Taylor Hill Road and then up the work road. The worst section was the long curve below Taylor Hill Road where Tink Smith and Ralph Rawson were stationed with jeeps to haul cars through the deep mud. Jessie Snyder's diary

Lowell Thomas, a friend of Frank Snyder's, visits the new ski area in 1962.

tells the story of those closing days of Stratton's first season:

> "Friday, March 30: Spring is upon us. I skied in shirt sleeves. It was water skiing on Stratton. The Board of Directors wrestled all day with whether to close.
>
> "Saturday, March 31: Rain, warm. The access road fell apart. In spite of it, 600 or 700 got to Stratton. Broke gas line on Oldsmobile—so I never got there.
>
> "Saturday, April 7: Pouring rain—a sombre situation for Stratton. Had 1½-hour lesson with Toni Egger.
>
> "Sunday, April 8: A lovely, last day of skiing at Stratton. We had a class with Walter (Heigl) in PM. Skiing still very enjoyable but running water everywhere."

Two days later, they yielded to Mother Nature and closed.

Early Struggles

There had been 65,000 "skier-day" visits, total receipts of $461,149, and they had almost broken even. But they had sold only half of the debentures.

Now followed an anxious debate. Should they shut down tight, the way Bromley did, keeping only three or four people on the payroll? If they did that, they would almost certainly turn a solid profit next year.

But this meant leaving Stratton half-finished. Each of the department heads had already submitted long lists of improvements that they felt were absolutely necessary. Most important of all—if they were to shut down, lock the door, and turn the key, they would lose their best people; and on one thing they were unanimous: Stratton was going to have to provide year-round employment for its people.

So they decided to maintain a skeleton summer staff and go ahead with the improvements, even though it wasn't clear where the money was coming from. It was another gamble, but they were getting used to gambling now. As of June 30, they had only $15,000 cash and receivables of $32,000 against payables of $217,000. They had now borrowed $700,000 of the $750,000 available from National Commercial, so they were technically insolvent. Their only hope was to sell the debentures.

Here they were once again to be disappointed. All summer and fall, cocktail parties and dinners were held to promote debentures, but not a single one was sold until October. People apparently forget about skiing after Easter and don't start thinking about it again until November.

The summer of 1962 was difficult—one of many still to come. A few things were accomplished, though. The state finished the access road, and it was a beautiful experience to drive on smooth pavement over the foothills and see Stratton Mountain for the first time from this vantage point. Morrissey finished the base lodge amid disputes about billing. Gillis built the Wanderer trail and a summit shelter. Sixteen private chalets were completed in the base area, bringing the total up to 20.[7] A group of Bostonians—Arthur Lee, Pat Grant, and Bill Tyler—built the 70-room Stratton Mountain Inn and had it ready for occupancy by December. Finally, Ed and Elinor Janeway had Ted Hunter draw up plans for a tiny 12-room auberge for Anne and Emo Henrich, which they were going to call "Birkenhaus."

Winter came early in 1962. Stratton opened on Saturday, December 8, with 200 skiers. Good snowfalls followed, with Christmas week starting off even better than in 1961. A blizzard laid down 20 inches of snow on December 29. Conditions were excellent on December 30, but then things fell apart. The cold front which followed the December 29 storm brought an "Arctic Fog" with it. This is a curious phenomenon which happens only in very cold, dry weather in snow-covered areas. As the snow in the ground sublimates (that is, evaporates), it almost immedately re-condenses in the air, forming tiny ice crystals. The effect can be the same as in ocean fog. Visibility gradually closes down, until it is hard to see more than 100 feet.

The night of December 30 was bitter cold. When the sun rose the next day, it was invisible in the fog, and the temperature in front of the base lodge had plunged to 28° below zero. All lifts opened on schedule at 8:00 AM, but, concerned about safety, Elmer Argast telephoned the summit and asked the summit lift operator to check the temperature on his newly installed thermometer.

"Fifty-five degrees below zero."

"That can't be right. Go out and check it again."

The answer came back the second time: 55° below zero. Wind speed was about 30 miles an hour, making for a wind-chill factor of 85°/118° below zero on the summit!

Elmer immediately passed word to close down all lifts. The trails were swept and buttoned down by 9:00 AM, long before most skiers arrive. Very few people complained about that decision!

On the next day, Old Man Winter relented a little. Temperatures rose to 10° below at the base and 28° below at the summit. For the handful of skiers who braved these conditions, repeated announcements were made over the base lodge public-address system warning against frostbite. Nevertheless, quite a number reported to First Aid with frozen noses and cheeks. The frigid air laid in the valley for another three days, pretty much ruining what would have otherwise been a perfect Christmas holiday. It was the only time in 20 years of operation that Stratton has had to shut down because of cold weather and, of course, receipts suffered.

Two weeks later, Lowell Thomas was making his annual tour through New England and stopped in at Stratton. Riding with him on the chair lift, Snyder told about the cold wave.

"What day was that?" Lowell asked.

"New Year's Eve."

"I was in Antarctica that week, and, on the 31st, we were all flown to the South Pole for the ceremony relieving Admiral Ducek of command. Of course, it's mid-summer down there, but the temperature was only about 20° below zero. So, it was colder at Stratton than at the South Pole that day!"

Lowell had taken to skiing on Clif Taylor's "shortee" skis. In those days, everyone felt they had to use seven footers, but Lowell much enjoyed demonstrating how easy it was to handle skies less than half as long. One of his old friends was Bill Parish, who owned Johnny Seesaw's over on Bromley Mountain, and it wasn't long before he had Bill talking up short skis with his customers. A year later, the idea was picked up by *SKI Magazine,* which convinced Karl Pfeiffer, who was then ski school director at Killington, to give lessons on short skis. The result was the now famous GLM method of teaching. But it should be remembered that the idea originally sprang from the fertile mind of Clif Taylor of Brattleboro, Vermont, and that one of skiing's great pioneers—Lowell Thomas—was instrumental in popularizing them.

In March, Stratton hosted its first professional ski race. Friedl Pfeiffer, one of Aspen's founders, had started an organization which he named the "International Professional Ski Racers' Association" (IPSRA). The racers were all ex-Olympians, having competed at the Squaw Valley Winter Games. IPSRA was in its second year and was having trouble gaining public acceptance. But the price was

[7] The first 16 chalet owners were: Dr. Pinckney Phyfe, Mr. and Mrs. William Mason, Mr. and Mrs. Douglas Mabee, Mr. and Mrs. Robert Pluff, Senator and Mrs. Edward Janeway, Mr. and Mrs. Frank Snyder, Mr. and Mrs. Edward Scheu, Mr. and Mrs. David Babbott, Dr. and Mrs. William Wawro, Mr. and Mrs. Willard Kiggins, Mr. and Mrs. Kenneth Ives, Mr. and Mrs. John Shuell, Mr. and Mrs. Bayard Ewing, Dr. and Mrs. George Gildea, Mr. and Mrs. Joseph Marcola, and Mrs. Claire Moorehead.

reasonable, and Stratton was looking for some easy publicity.

A giant slalom was set from the summit to the base down North American and Suntanner. Great and famous skiers participated: Christian Pravda, Ernst Hinterseer, Adrien Duvillard, Hias Leitner, Anderl Molterer, Pepi Gramshammer, and Othmar Schneider. Christian Pravda had the best time.—2 minutes 20 seconds. Toni Lechner, otherwise known as "Fat Toni," the happy schuhplatter dancer and Stratton ski instructor, competed and, to everyone's surprise, posted good time, walking off with some of the prize money!

New Lifts, Trails—A Chapel

When the snow melted in April and the directors had totaled up the results, they felt that, at last, they were over the hump. Sales had been almost double the previous year. Debentures had sold well. Payables had been reduced and were current. Best of all, there was a healthy bank balance. It was time to

The Inns at Stratton Mountain

Stratton's original land use plan called for the construction of only four inns in the base area and four were constructed in time. The first was named the "Stratton Mountain Inn," a motel-like structure which was built by a young hotelier from Boston by the name of Arthur Lee. Lee owned and operated a successful operation on the then new Route 128 that went around Boston and it was called the "128 Motel." The new Inn at Stratton was designed along similar Spartan lines. The emphasis was to be on plenty of rooms and minimum public areas.

The Inn had several rough seasons at the beginning, but then Dave Clark, a Cornell graduate in hotel management, was brought in to be manager. From that day on the Inn's fortunes slowly but steadily improved. When Arthur Lee died in 1965, his brother William Lee, along with partner Patrick Grant, continued to operate the Inn until 1976 when they sold the operation to the Stratton Corporation. In February of 1979, the Inn's attractive 32-room annex called Windham House was completed. Its 250-seat auditorium and "break-out" meeting rooms provided a needed flexibility for booking combinations of meetings, and helped to increase convention business. The present manager is Dave Eastlake.

At the time of the opening of Stratton Mountain Ski Area, Ed and Elinor Janeway decided they would like to build a small inn for the new ski school director, Emo Henrich, and his wife Ann. The matter was discussed and the Henrichs agreed it was a great idea. After a drawing had been made by Emo of what the inn should look like, both inside and out, it was given to Ted Hunter, an architect and former U.S. Olympic skier. Hunter then designed the inn that would be called "Birkenhaus"—the name in English means birch tree house. It opened in December 1962, with only four double rooms, two bunk rooms and a dining room with two long tables. Everyone sat together family style. Today Birkenhaus can accommodate between 50 and 60 guests for sleeping, and more than that in the much enlarged dining area. The Henrichs are now studying plans for a further expansion. Meanwhile, Birkenhaus has become one of the social centers of the Mountain. Ann is a great organizer of parties, and guests as well as friends and neighbors find themselves happily involved in all kinds of celebrations—whether it is an indoor Easter Egg Hunt, an Austrian Fasching costume party or someone's special birthday.

Next door is the Liftline Lodge, which is owned by a group of Massachusetts investors, headed by Dr. George Gildea, a stockholder of Stratton Corporation and Tink Smith's brother-in-law. Liftline has been well managed since it opened for the 1963–1964 season by Herbert Schachinger and his capable wife, Gretel.

Like the other inns, Liftline has constantly expanded and now has two attractive connecting buildings—Glockenhoff and Berghaus. The architecture, atmosphere and cuisine are all reminiscent of Schachinger's home town of Bad Gastein. If you can catch "Herbie" long enough to have a small visit with him, you will find a most congenial man who is interesting and knowledgeable about many things. He is definitely good company.

In 1968 a Peru, Vermont resident and Stratton supporter, John Shuell, decided to back Walter Heigl, an Austrian ski instructor, and build the fourth inn. Shuell enlisted the support of eight other investors who were persuaded that there was a need for another facility. It was named "Hotel Tyrol" and went up right alongside Birkenhaus. It operated for several years and then was leased, and later purchased in 1975 by the Ski Educational Foundation, for use of The Stratton Mountain School.

think about expansion again, and they decided to tackle two projects: more lifts and trails, and a chapel.

Ski school had tripled the number of lessons, and both Emo Henrich and Gene Gillis were asking for more novice teaching slopes. Fortunately, good terrain existed to the left of the lower Tamarack. Gene designed two novice slopes (Daniel Webster and Bear Cub) and two T-bar lifts were ordered from Hall Ski Lift Co. for $57,000. (Over Elmer Argast's objection, it should be recorded. He far preferred another chair lift. As matters turned out, he was correct, but the Directors felt there wasn't enough money.)

The Chapel was Tink Smith's project. Sandy McIlvaine donated the design—a beautiful one which was to be much admired over the years. Peter Butinsky of Brattleboro, received the contract for $50,000, and ground was broken in early June.

During the summer, work progressed smoothly on the new slopes. Steel for the new lifts arrived on time. By October, the novice slopes, two T-bars, and a new expert run (the Spruce), were completed and ready for skiers well ahead of time.

At the Annual Corporation Meeting in October, Smith and Snyder changed jobs—Tink becoming President and Frank becoming Chairman. The reason was simple—Frank's New York partners felt that he should back out of Stratton's operations and spend more time at Moore & Munger's affairs.

Going into the third season, Stratton's General Manager, Elmer Argast, was having health problems. After a serious operation he returned to work, but his working relationship with department heads—and with the Board—was steadily deteriorating. He left the company early in January, with Tink Smith taking over the added responsibility of General Manager. Elmer had done a wonderful job at Stratton. The area probably could not have opened in 1961 without his patient bulldogging, and it couldn't have been built better by anyone else.

For the third straight year, the snow gods were kind. Total snowfall was 190 inches, with virtually no rain, and Stratton experienced another surge in sales and profits.

By March 1964, it looked as though the Company would have $450,000 to spend on expansion. All fall and winter, they had been studying how to finance and build a golf course. At the same time, Gene Gillis had been cruising the northside gully, which, years ago, Bob Wright had predicted would provide good expert skiing.

In June 1964, the construction work started again, and it was another stupendous summer. On the mountain, two new runs were cut (Liftline and Slalom Glade), and a new 5,100-foot Heron double chair (the Snow Bowl) ordered and erected. In the base area, Tink Smith supervised the clearing, dozing, and completion of the first nine holes of the golf course. Again, weather was kind; there was very little rain to hinder construction.

On October 10, another major event took place: the first Annual Stratton Festival of the Arts. Sponsored jointly with the Stratton Corporation and the Vermont Arts and Crafts Council, the Festival was designed to promote Vermont art and artists. Among the many public-spirited persons who helped launch this effort were Elinor Janeway and Kay Smith.

At the annual stockholder meeting that year, the Board reported total revenues of $1,169,900, an increase of 42.6% over 1963, with earnings of $132,390. The debenture issue had finally been sold out, and the bonds were now selling at a premium.

Stratton was on the move, and the future looked rosy.

Stratton Pioneers a Snowmaking System

But all was not rosy. Nature, which had been kind to the Stratton developers over the last three years, now took a big swipe at them. The resort had opened as usual early in December, and a nice 16-inch base had built up, with better skiing conditions than in previous years at this time. Then, on December 23, a tropical storm moved in from the Bermuda Triangle. A temperature inversion developed—always a bad sign for eastern ski areas—and, early on December 24, the downpour began. By Christmas morning, hardly a vestige of snow was left on the mountain, and Stratton had to shut down. It was little consolation that every other New England ski area was in the same boat. Stratton was to remain closed for 27 days.

John Mathiewson of Larchmont Engineering was called in, and a plan was quickly drawn up to provide snowmaking on the Suntanner and Tyrolienne. The equipment was delivered on January 14. Tink Smith and his men worked overtime all the next week. By January 23, Stratton had enough man-made and natural snow cover, and the area was reopened to the public. By February 1, good conditions existed all over the mountain, when another storm just like the first one struck, this time leaving the mountain sheathed in two inches of clear, blue ice. Tink and Gene had just developed an ice chopper something like a roto-tiller, and the new machine was put to work. By February 15, much of the ice had been chewed up, and—with the help of snowmaking—conditions were good once more. Stratton was gaining a reputation in the East for

The Stratton Arts Festival

In the summer of 1963 a rather unique venture for a ski area was started. Elinor Janeway, a member of the Vermont Arts and Crafts Commission, and Kay Smith, both wives of original Directors of the Stratton Corporation, felt there was an opportunity to demonstrate the fine work being done by Vermont artists and craftsmen. What better place to launch such a venture than the new Base Lodge on Stratton Mountain for the Columbus Day weekend? The Stratton Corporation enthusiastically agreed it was worth a try.

Under the expert guidance of Peter Wendland, who had grown up on the mountain, walking the six long miles to school, a skilled craftsman himself and at that time Executive Director of the Arts and Crafts Service, the first Stratton Arts Festival opened with the mountain a blaze of fall color. Several eager volunteers ably assisted in displaying the work of 30 exhibitors in the west wing. A small commission was charged but there was no charge for admission. (Perhaps a reason for the startling success of that first Festival as Vermonters and travellers came to see and to buy!)

Now, 18 years later, it is amazing and rather difficult to recall the phases of growth to its present size and reputation. The generous support of the Stratton Corporation made it possible to plan a more ambitious Festival. A Board of Trustees was formed and before long the Stratton Arts Festival was duly incorporated as a non-profit organization. "Non-Profit" was indeed a true description of the early years. As the show became widely known the number of exhibitors increased dramatically and before long two floors of the Base Lodge, so familiar to skiers, were transformed for four weeks. The Vermont Council of the Arts awarded grants and a growing list of enthusiastic patrons were responsible for putting the Festival on a sound financial basis. However without the assistance of a large group of volunteers there would be no Festival. With a slight profit realized in the last few years a Scholarship Fund was established to honor outstanding participants. Children from many schools are admitted without charge during the week under the stimulating guidance of their teachers.

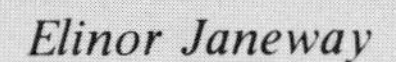

Elinor Janeway

Kay Smith

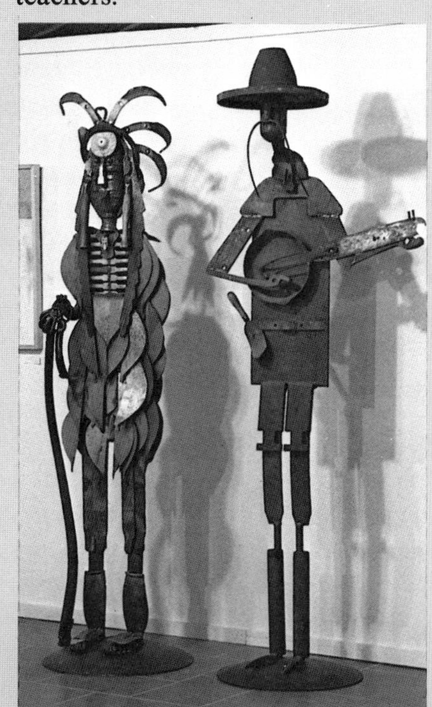

Demonstrations of various skills have become an increasing attraction of the weekend programs. Most importantly, the Performing Arts have brought highly talented representatives to Stratton. Recently a young pianist from the famous Marlboro Festival, Cecile Licad from the Philippines gave a brilliant recital. In recognition of her extraordinary talent she has just received the coveted Leventritt Award enabling her to appear as a soloist with the New York Philharmonic and to be a recording artist. Outstanding groups presented ballet programs, mimes and puppet shows. For several years the Vermont Symphony has found enthusiastic audiences at Stratton.

It would be impossible to name all the Directors who have created their individual effects of the annual Festival. But in 1981 most special mention should be made of Hubert Schriebl and his talented, tireless team of assistants who so ably displayed the works of three hundred talented Vermonters. No other ski area has yet ventured to demonstrate that there is this much more than skiing to a mountain.

snow grooming, and skiers flocked to the area during February and March. To everyone's surprise, the season ended slightly ahead of 1963/64.

Meanwhile, in recognition of their efforts through this difficult period, two of Stratton's most loyal employees were given promotions by the Board: Mitch McLaughlin to General Manager at a salary of $12,000, and Roland Scott to Controller at $8,400—pretty good numbers for those days!

Summer, 1965, was a season for retrenchment, but some things simply had to be done: a new ski patrol house was desperately needed on the summit; the Slalom Glade and Liftline trails had to be seeded; and, most important of all, the new snowmaking system had to be rebuilt on a permanent basis, with electric compressors housed in the base lodge.

In the base area, real estate development continued at the same steady pace as in previous years: 20 new chalets and 24 cooperative row houses. A fourth inn—Hotel Tyrol—was constructed, and clearing was begun on the second nine holes of the golf course.

The 1965 Annual Report recorded total receipts of $1,343,030 and net earnings of $57,121. Concluding their annual message to the stockholders, Smith and Snyder wrote:

> "In five short years, Stratton has succeeded in reaching most of its original objectives. These were: to build a major ski facility of the highest quality; a ski school which is looked upon as the East's best; a chalet area which would offer zoning protection, privacy and complete utility service; and, finally, a golf course for summer vacationers. The golf course and lake are well on their way to completion. Only two things are lacking from the basic master plan: construction of the Village, and a second lift from the base area to a point above mid-station. If the 1966 and 1967 seasons are a success, the master plan may be completed over the next two summers.
>
> "The Village will consist of . . . drug, grocery, sports, milk bar, arts and crafts, restaurant, and post office. Automobile travel will be prohibited."

It would have amazed them then to know that 16 years were to pass before a start would be made on the Village.

Stability: The Ski Resort Established

The 1965/66 season began with a warm Christmas, temperatures in the 40's, and little snow. On New Year's Day, the temperature had risen to the 50's, and it looked as though a wash-out was in progress which would wreck still another holiday week. But, on Sunday, January 2, a big snow storm blew in, dumping over a foot of snow. From that point on, blizzard followed blizzard, and Stratton enjoyed the best season yet in its brief history.

By March, a record season was coming to a close, and on March 26, the Board met to decide what improvements to make during the summer. As in previous years, they were unanimous that all profits would be applied either to reducing bank debt or to plant expansion. (However, small dividends were declared during the years 1971 to 1973.)

The procedure followed in 1966 set a pattern for later years: management prepared a shopping list of capital improvements, starting with the most urgent item at the top of the list and running down through items of decreasing importance—each with an estimated cost set down. In 1965, seven items had been requested. The board voted four and ended up with one: No. 5 Standard Chairlift, as the estimated cost would exceed slightly the $250,000 of available money.

Chair Lift No. 5 was to be another Heron double. The loading station was designed to be in the base area right next to Chair Lift No. 1 (the Suntanner lift). The unloading station was located higher than the Suntanner lift's upper terminal, so that skiers could reach the North American lift without having to walk or climb.

A major new trail was planned from the summit. It was to be an easy intermediate run that would curve around towards the east before coming down the ridge that separates the northeast face of the mountain from the east face. On March 27, a new six-inch snowfall made for ideal bushwacking conditions, an unbreakable crust under the new snow, making it possible to move easily through the woods. So, Mitch McLaughlin, Karl Bauer, Casey Rowley, and Frank Snyder packed light lunches and headed for the summit. As they started down the route of the new trail, "center-lining" it with red plastic ribbons every 30 feet or so, the sun broke through, turning it into a beautiful day.

They hadn't gone 200 yards before they began to see bear tracks—not just one or two, but what looked like a whole convention of bears—large tracks, middle-sized, and small ones—everywhere they looked. In his usual cheerful way, Mitch suggested that they "move right along," and so they did, nervously looking into the bush for signs of black bear.

As they broke out of the tight summit spruce-tree jungle, they reached a flat area with no sign of bear anywhere. Here stood a single giant spruce. Taking off their skis, they stopped for a bite of lunch, and a beer. Then they climbed up the tree to have a look around. It was their first view of the east side of the

The Stratton Courtesy Patrol is formed: from left to right, Octave Gisquet, Ski Patrol Director Casey Rowley, Phil Snyder, Frank Snyder, Ted Montague, unidentified NSP representative, Warren Hellman, Danny Davison, Win Taylor, Bob Pluff, Ev Herre, and Win Hoyt.

mountain and what is now called the "Sun Bowl."

After lunch, they finished the center-lining job. When the trail had been cut and bulldozed later that year, it was appropriately named "Black Bear." The spot where they had halted for lunch and a beer is at the beginning of the Downeaster trail, where it takes off from Black Bear—a location that has been called the "Beer Can Point" by Casey and his patrolmen ever since.

Much other work was done that summer. The Hemlock and White Birch trails were finished, making it easy to reach the Snow Bowl lift from the top of chair lift No. 5. Four of the second nine golf holes were cut, and the west wing extension of the base lodge was completed on schedule.

The 1966/67 season began with opening day on December 3 in good snow conditions. A spate of warm weather followed, wiping out all the natural snow by mid-month. Once again, the New England ski areas were facing a grim Christmas holiday week when on December 24, they received a beautiful Christmas present in the form of 28 inches of snow.

What followed was another excellent season. The Black Bear trail lived up to expectations, immediately becoming the most popular run on the mountain. Amateur and professional races were held successfully, and the U.S. Ski Team trained happily on the mountain, giving the Stratton juniors a close-up of big time amateur racing.

During the summer, Karl Bauer laid out and completed two new trails between Black Bear and Tamarack—they were named Polar Bear and Grizzly Bear. The sewage treatment plant was modified to meet new state water-quality standards. The first four holes of the second nine holes of the golf course were completed, and the first nine "village chalets" were built just downhill from the chapel.

Sel Hannah was hired to lay out a new set of trails on the east side of the mountain using detailed contour maps, which Stratton had made by stereoptic airplane photography. Sel cruised the mountain during the early summer. The base area, he was convinced, should be about one mile south of the present base. From there, at elevation 2,000 feet, the terrain climbed smoothly to a flat area 1,200 feet above the base. He proposed a 4,400 ft. chair lift to run between these points. The skiing would be most intermediate and would be much warmer, he felt. There was one drawback, though; the terrain would not permit a second lift to run to the summit from the unloading point. This area was to be named the Sun Bowl a year later.

At the stockholders meeting in October, management reported sales of $1,879,249 and earnings of $197,800—the best year yet in Stratton's history.

The 1967/68 season was in many ways a repeat of the previous year. Stratton opened on December 2 and sailed through a record-breaking Christmas–New Year week. There was the usual January thaw, followed by the coldest February yet, with no new snow at all.

The U.S. Olympic Team arrived March 1 on its way home from Grenoble to compete in the only post-Olympics competition in this country. There wasn't a great deal of cover on the mountain at the time, but a big storm blew through on the first, dropping 16 inches of fresh powder. Volunteers, ski patrolmen, and ski instructors spent much of the day footpacking Liftline and Spruce, the two trails that had been set aside for the races.

These were held in zero temperatures, but the conditions were superb, and Stratton was complimented by the officials for having organized a first-rate competition.

Spring followed right behind the March 3 cold front and, from that day to the end of the season four weeks later, the temperature never again dipped below freezing. March, which is usually the biggest month of the season, turned out to be a disaster. Stratton finally closed on March 31, having counted 132,501 skier days. In spite of the disappointing spring holiday period, it had been the second largest season to date.

Because of the early spring, woodcutters were able to begin trail clearing in the Sun Bowl in mid-March. Seventy-five acres of trails had now been planned, with four trails, later to be named Sunriser, Sundowner, Downeaster, and Gentle Ben. A sixth lift was ordered from Bob Heron, this one 4,400 feet long and 1,200 feet vertical. Snowmaking was expanded on the lower Standard trail, and the last five holes of the golf course were completed.

Harvey Clifford Takes Over

In October, 1968, Tink Smith retired for personal reasons, and Harvey Clifford was brought in as President and Chief Executive. When the news was announced, Mitch McLaughlin resigned. Perhaps Mitch felt that he had earned his chance at the top job and that now was a good time to start his own consulting firm. His easy and pleasant manner had been a great asset to the Company, and he would be missed. A few weeks later, Irene Benson decided to retire. It was the biggest personnel change yet to hit the Company, and Fall, 1968, was a period of doubt and uncertainty among Stratton's employees.

Harvey Clifford, the man who was coming in to take over, had impressive credentials. Excellent skier (a former member of the Canadian Olympic team), ski coach, ski school director, and, finally, General Manager at Stratton's neighbor and competitor, the Mt. Snow Development Corp., he had experienced just about all of the problems that beset ski areas, and he had built a fine reputation as an administrator.

His style could not have been more of a contrast from Smith's and McLaughlin's. Whereas they were folksy and outgoing, he was reserved; where they often dispensed with corporate organization to get a job done quickly, he soon had the employees reor-

"Tink" Smith enjoys his game: the course is completed.

ganized with precise lines of responsibility and authority.

Clifford's first problem, however, was mechanical. In March, the decision had been made to delay maintenance and replacement of the snow grooming equipment, with the inevitable result that, when the snows came and the ski area opened on November 16, breakdowns were frequent. Clifford promptly arranged for delivery of new snow cats, and, by early January, the snow grooming operation was functioning well again.

Nature was kind that winter of 1968/69. Except for the usual January thaws, conditions were the best that Stratton had ever experienced, and, when the area closed on April 18 after 154 days of operation, the numbers looked good. By June 30—the end of the fiscal year—total revenue was a record $2.8 million and net earnings at $142,805.

The 1968/69 season saw the creation of three more new institutions on the Mountain; the first annual Ski Ball, an early March extravaganza benefit, was organized and run by Peggy Lord and Eugenie Greeff (with the able assistance of Ernie Greeff). It was a great success and was to become a major event every year thereafter. Another new organization, the Ski Educational Foundation, was the brainchild of Warren Hellman, Chairman of Lehman Brothers and a Stratton chalet owner, who had taken over the junior racing program, just as its founder, Lloyd Clark, was succumbing to a long, unsuccessful battle with diabetes. Under Hellman's dynamic leadership, Stratton's junior racing program soon became the East's best.

The third institution was the new Arnold Palmer Golf Academy. Clifford signed a five-year franchise agreement with Arnold Palmer Enterprises for the exclusive right to operate a golf academy in New England. Geoffrey Cornish was retained to create a training site on the field behind the old Sally Day farm house on Taylor Hill Road.[8]

Summer 1969 was another season of heavy construction. As Tink Smith was to say over and over: Stratton wasn't really a ski area, it was a long-term building project. In addition to the extensive maintenance, projects brought to completion this year were: the second nine golf holes, two ski trails (upper Downeaster and Slalom Glade), and the first nine "Village Chalets". The latter were Stratton's first venture into cluster housing, an approach to medium density housing that was new at this time. Plans called for twenty-seven of them.

During his first six months at the helm, Clifford had moved quickly to reorganize management. Craig Swart was transferred from the Cashier's office to take over the growing Real Estate Department, replacing Ev Herre, who had gone to Bromley. Although this was a new field for Craig, he was to do a superb job and was to earn the love and respect of Stratton's chalet owners. John Layman was hired from Mt. Snow to fill a new slot: that of Chief Engineer and Project Manager. A precise and thorough British ex-naval officer, Layman set right to work reorganizing the engineering office.

After having supported Stratton from the very beginning, Peter Pappas decided that it was time to concentrate his efforts at his Paradise Restaurant in Bennington, and both he and his brother-in-law, Jimmie Pleyotis, now resigned, to everyone's regret. Clifford now hired Moe Mozier to take over Stratton's restaurant and cafeteria. Moe quickly became known as the "King of the Ski Bums". He used them almost everywhere, hiring them in the mornings and giving them day passes. He had a great way with the young people—his gleaming bald head and bushy mustache being instantly identifiable from a distance. But, each winter—along with the snowshoe hares—Moe would also put on a winter coat. It was a thick hair piece, which completely altered his appearance, thereby confusing more than a few folks on the Mountain.

Also among the new arrivals that summer: Dick McLernon, who took over as Marketing Director, and Elmer Reed, the new golf professional. Dick stayed only a few months and was followed by Dick Lechthaler, who was to be Marketing Director for the next six years.

In retrospect, that first year of Clifford's administration was one of Stratton's best. In 1969, directors were: Philip K. Allen, Harvey F. Clifford, A. Luke Crispe, Edward G. Janeway, John O. Morris, Robert E. Pluff, Herbert O. Smith, Nelson M. Smith, E. Philip Snyder Jr., and Frank V. Snyder. All of the original problems of ten years ago had been met and overcome. The Company was on a sound financial basis; sales were growing; the lifts and trails were great, and the skiing being offered was among the best in the East. The problems discussed in Board meetings that summer were routine—such as whether to refinance the Company's $1.2 million long-term debt to eliminate the usual $300,000 working capital loans (which was done) and whether to raise the all-day adult ski ticket price to the unprecedented level of $10 (also done).

The future looked secure. They were confident that, if they watched costs, continued to reduce debt and kept on building the trail and lift systems, while slowly expanding the residential "chalet area," they would just be continuing a proven formula of success. At the same time, they recognized that they

[8] Construction was completed by October, 1970. The Academy opened for business in May, 1971.

Social Life on the Mountain

A sparkling social life developed in the 1960's and included the Stratton Ski Ball: (left to right from top) Mr. & Mrs. Arthur Over, Mr. & Mrs. Douglas Melville with Mr. & Mrs. George Reichhelm, Mr. & Mrs. Charles Sonnenfeld, Mr. & Mrs. Rex Marshall, Mrs. DeSpirlet & Louis Cabot, Eugenie Greeff & Warren Hellman, Dean McKay & Lucy Lieder, Ernie Greeff & Peggy Lord, Mr. & Mrs. Stig Albertsson, Mrs. Gordon Calder. Bart & Steffie Jacobs at "birthday inn" Birkenhaus. Benzi Henrich & Octave Gisquet model at annual Norse House fashion show.

would have to develop summer activities in order to attract real estate sales and to support the four base area inns. So, to reorganize and recast their thinking, they hired a bright, young architect by the name of Whitney Delnoce Goubert to prepare a new long-range plan. When completed, the Goubert plan called for a steady expansion of the skiing facilities, a village "hub" to be located just above the main parking lot, and a development plan for the real estate in the Sun Bowl. Since the latter property was under lease with International Paper, Goubert's plan called for a joint venture in the Sun Bowl between IP and Stratton.

To support this development plan, two additional lifts were planned in the Sun Bowl, along with a base lodge. One would go up White Birch Hill, a southeast-facing novice slope just above and to the right of the existing Sun Bowl base area; a second, longer lift would take skiers to the north summit of the Mountain, loading at a point about one mile to the south of the Sun Bowl lift upper terminal. It was felt that the novice lift (up what was later to be named "Big Ben") would tie in with construction of condominiums along that slope to provide "ski-in," "ski-out" housing, something rare at American ski areas.

Environmental Problems Arise

While these optimistic plans were being set to paper, no one at Stratton realized that serious trouble was brewing. Vietnam war protests were beginning to shake the Country; the "counter-culture," with its emphasis on drugs and anti-establishmentarianism, was blossoming. Hippie colonies were springing up even in Vermont; "environmental protection" (a new phrase) and "ecology" (an old one) were coming into popularity and would soon bring forth much needed new legislation, some of which would create problems for ski areas like Stratton.

Late in the previous year, International Paper Corp. had purchased a Michigan land development company known as American Central Corp. Being the largest private landowner in the U.S.—with a million or so acres (about the size of the State of Ohio) IP felt that they should participate in the booming land development business by using some properties that were not of prime importance for wood pulp.

One piece of land so selected bordered on Stratton: the 500-acre tract abutting on the Access Road and extending across solid woodlands (some of it close to 2,500 feet in elevation) which surround Gulf Brook, Mud Pond, and the old trail leading from Grahamville to Stratton Pond.

In April, 1970, American Central's President, Don Foote, notified Stratton that this area had been selected for development.

Meanwhile, a big brouhaha was breaking out in Wilmington, 18 miles to the south. There, a new ski area, Haystack, had sold a large number of lots without sewer lines or treatment plant and had then run into trouble with town authorities. Now the developers were locked in legal battle with the Town, a battle that Haystack was not going to win and which would finally lead it to bankruptcy.

It was not long before the State got into the act: Ed Janeway, who was senior State Senator for the County, invited Governor Deane Davis to come down for a first hand look. The Governor came and he was shocked at the strip development that had sprung up along Route 100 between Wilmington and West Dover.

"I can't believe I'm still in Vermont," he kept saying, as he drove by the motels, ski shops, and fast food shops of Mt. Snow's "Valley of the Inns."

He threw his powerful support behind the environmentalists, who had been struggling to get what they called an "environmental control bill" through the State legislature.

A few months later, the environmental control bill passed both houses and was signed into law. "Act 250," as it was called, was landmark legislation, soon to receive nationwide publicity.

So far, Stratton Corp. had been untouched by these developments (although its time was coming). Fiscal 1970 had turned out to be essentially a repeat of 1969. Sales were the same: $2.8 million, but earnings had risen to a record $207,981, making it the best financial year yet. Over $679,000 had been invested in new capital projects and yet the Company was again able to reduce bank debt.

By now, the Stratton chalet area had grown to 2,-000 beds, with another 350 commercial beds at the inns. Compared to the big western resorts, this was small potatoes—Aspen was advertising 50,000 beds and an expansion rate of 2,000 beds a year, while Vail, which had opened one year later than Stratton was growing even faster than that. Even so, a few Vermonters were beginning to view Stratton with a critical eye. Was this really Vermont?

Meanwhile, Clifford sat down with Bob Andrews of American Central, and tried to sell him on a joint venture over in the Sun Bowl. Andrews was mildly interested and agreed to hire a land planner to look over the site. David Jay Flood was hired and promptly set to work. His qualifications were excellent; he had done all the planning and architecture at Sun Valley after Bill Janss had bought it, and he was also working for Keystone, another major new Colorado resort, laying out their village and hotel.

Flood's approach was far different from Goubert's. Since his office was in Los Angeles, he worked only from topographic maps. Maximum concentration at the base area was his credo. The Flood Plan called for a walk-through village in the Sun Bowl, along with 1,400 condominium units. The Stratton people objected to this heavy concentration of beds. Nevertheless, negotiations proceeded, and on June 12, Stratton's Board approved of a twelve point proposal to be submitted to IP.

Andrews submitted a counter-proposal in September. It would extend Stratton's lease for 25 years but modified the lease to exclude the 782 acres in the Sun Bowl (which would now be deeded to American Central). Stratton's lease would be extended by 197 acres to permit Stratton to expand its trail system on the Mountain, and Stratton would agree to build four more chair lifts.

It was a tough counter and one which would have totally excluded Stratton from playing a part in the base area development. Nevertheless, it was not

Stratton Mountain School

"Stratton Mountain School is an ambitious attempt to give young American skiers opportunities to match those enjoyed by European competitors who ski and train year-round from their Alpine front porches. The U.S. Ski Educational Foundation, set up largely through private donations, is also an answer to almost every other skiing nation in the world whose governments operate or assist their competitive racing programs."

The New York Times Magazine
February 1981
Holcomb B. Noble

But in the beginning the concept was a modest one—just a simple tutoring program to help a few enthusiastic skiing youngsters to keep up in their school work. It originated in the mind of Donald Tarinelli, at that time a building contractor from Fairfield, Connecticut, and Warren Hellman, an investment banker from New York City. Both men had children involved in the ski racing program, and they soon realized that the combination of weekend racing in Vermont and Monday morning classes back in their schools in Connecticut or New York was resulting in educational disaster. It was then they decided to hire a tutor for the winter months, and ask other parents to join in. They wound up with three tutors, a coach and 12 kids. The girls stayed at the Tarinelli chalet and the boys at the Hellmans'—and that was 10 years ago.

Eventually the school acquired the unused Hotel Tyrol, once a ski lodge, and turned it into classrooms and living quarters for the approximately 70 students. It has become fully accredited, and with a staff of 11 teachers, 9 coaches, and the headmaster, is producing students who are strong academically and who are also great skiers.

In 1977, the Stratton Corporation's lease was coming up for renewal with International Paper Company which owned a part of Stratton Mountain's acreage. Tarinelli, now the Stratton Corporation president, and Hellman, the President of the U.S. Ski Educational Foundation (the organization which does the funding for the U.S. Ski Team), worked together on an arrangement that would guarantee the school's future and also the future of the Stratton Corporation. It was Tarinelli's idea and the proposal was: International Paper would make a tax deductible gift of the leased lands to the U.S. Ski Educational Foundation; who in turn would give the Stratton Corporation a 99 year lease in exchange for a fair annual rent. It was a good solution to a number of problems, and the paper company agreed. When the final details were worked out, all concerned were happy that the school could continue to do its outstanding job with some financial security.

The effectiveness of the school is apparent by the number of graduates currently considered world-class skiers, such as Mike Frost, a young Vermonter, who competed in the 1981 World Cup competition with the U.S. National Team and Heidi Preuss who placed fourth in the downhill event at the 1980 Olympics at Lake Placid. Altogether there is an impressive list of graduates and current students who are making a name for themselves and the school by their performances in both the Alpine and the cross-country events throughout the country. Its alumni are bound to provide some winners in future Olympics.

First Board of the newly established
Ski Educational Foundation
1971

OFFICERS
Mr. F. Warren Hellman—President
Mrs. Robert T. Middleton—Vice President
Mrs. Phyllis Schwartz—Secretary-Treasurer

DIRECTORS:
Mr. Paul E. Bedell, Jr.
Mrs. Harvey Clifford
Mr. Jack W. Frost
Mr. Ernest T. Greeff
Mr. Thomas F. Head, 3rd
Mr. Emo Henrich
Mr. Rex Marshall
Mr. Edward M. Scheu, Jr.
Mr. Nelson W. Smith
Mr. Frank V. Snyder
Mr. Donald Tarinelli

Executive Director—T. D. McCormick
Director of Racing—Herman Goellner

without precedent, this being the arrangement under which Aspen Ski Corp. and American Cement had just joined together to build Snowmass in Colorado. However, Stratton and American Central could not come to final agreement that Autumn, 1970, and through the following winter, the American Central people became even more discouraged about their prospects in Vermont.

In March 1971, Don Foote made the decision to move American Central out of Vermont, and he offered to sell approximately 1,000 acres of Sun Bowl land to Stratton for $1,300,000—$200,000 down and $100,000 per year for 11 years. Stratton now made a counter proposal, agreeing to the purchase price but demanding an extension of the lease for up to 86 years as a condition. Foote balked at this—IP's Woodlands department would have to approve of a lease extension, and they were refusing to budge.

Stratton's First Act 250 Hearing

By the end of the 1969/70 ski season, plans were finalized for the two new Sun Bowl lifts, and an application was filed with the District Environmental Commission under Act 250. The hearing was set for May 17.

Without realizing it, Stratton was about to become entangled in environmental problems. The first and most serious was the sewage treatment plant. As of mid-1970, this plant—one of the newest and best in the State—could not meet the new water quality standards which had just come into effect.

The reason was the passage, during the adjourned session of the Vermont legislature, of another landmark of environmental law—Act 250, which permitted the State's Water Resource Board to establish statewide water pollution regulations. When finalized, these new administrative rules made Stratton's sewage treatment plan illegal by providing that no one could discharge effluent into a mountain stream above 1,500 feet elevation unless the dilution rate was at the ratio of 1 gallon effluent to 30 gallons of stream water. There was really no way that this ratio could be met on Stratton Mountain at certain periods of low stream flow in August. In effect, while offering no acceptable alternative, the State had placed Stratton in an impossible situation.

Against this background, Stratton's management went to the hearing. These were the early days of Act 250 (this was the first petition to come before District Environmental Commission No. 1), and rules of procedure had yet to be formalized. As a result, almost everyone who lived down the road and who wanted to speak was given a chance.

The hearing dragged on for days, then weeks. Newspapers had a field day.

The permit was finally issued late in the summer, with three conditions attached: (1) that Stratton get clearance from the Department of Water Resources on its sewage treatment plant; (2) that Stratton file an acceptable plan for limiting attendance at the ski area; and (3) that the Town pass ordinances limiting parking on all roads in and around the Stratton ski area.

Stratton filed formal objections to the latter two conditions, on the theory that these were subjects beyond the scope of Act 250. Nevertheless, a ticket limitation plan was drafted anyway and implemented during the following season.

Meanwhile, Clifford began to meet with the Department of Water Resources people to see what kind of plant could be designed and built which would meet the tough new rules. Eventually, it was agreed that a tertiary[9] plant be designed with capacity to treat 300,000 gallons a day. The State would not yield on the prohibition against injection of effluent into the stream, and after many months of conferences, a system for offstream disposal (also known as "spray irrigation") worked out by which the effluent would be sprayed into the woods along the sixth hole of the golf course.

Construction was begun in 1971. (The plant was finally to cost almost $1 million.) At the same time that this work was proceeding, John Layman began a major overhaul of the utility lines throughout the area. There were many leaks, which were causing extensive infiltration of surface water into the sewer lines and which were seriously increasing the load on the treatment plant.

Environmental problems were coming down on the heads of many ski area operators in 1971 and 1972. So, at the suggestion of Steve Bradley (General Manager of the Winter Park Ski Area in Colorado), Frank Snyder (then President of the National Ski Areas Association) arranged for a three-day environmental seminar for all member ski areas to be held in June, 1972 at the Thorne Ecological Institute in Aspen, Colorado.

Over a hundred ski areas were represented at this gathering, along with officials from the U.S. Forest Service, and various State Environmental officers and including Vermont. After two days of outdoor classes, the group moved indoors to hear papers and to conclude the sessions. Two interesting conclusions were drawn in the final wrap-up meeting: (1) Dr. Thorne stated that in her opinion, the ski area operators attending this gathering were the most environmentally-informed executives that the Institute had ever encountered; (2) the Chief Forester for White Mountain National Forest (which is

[9] A tertiary sewage treatment plant is one which purifies the effluent so that it is safe for human consumption.

located in Colorado) stated that it was his opinion that the problem is not with the ski area operators but rather with the developers down the road who are not in it for the long haul but are just looking for quick profits. He knew of no way to control bad development down the road.

Certainly, the people at Stratton looked at it that way. They felt that they had done more planning and had been as careful to preserve the environment as any other ski area in New England and that they were being unfairly criticized for pollution and traffic congestion. They were determined to build the best sewage treatment plant in the State and said so, while at the same time, publicly supporting Act 250 and the State's efforts to control pollution.

By the end of summer 1972, Stratton's environmental problems were slowly ironing out, although at a very high cost to the Company. The Sun Bowl plans had to be shelved for that reason, even though the fiscal year had ended with record sales $3.3 million and earnings of $169,000.

Now followed two very poor seasons. The winter of 1972/73 brought marginal snow. As had happened in 1970, spring came early with temperatures never falling below freezing after March 2nd. Stratton closed on March 26th—the earliest closing in its history, with sales dropping to $2.9 million and earnings to zero. Expansion on the Mountain was out. All available capital funds now had to be channeled into completion of the sewage treatment plant, spray irrigation and sewer line renovation, and for necessary replacements on the Mountain.

In October, 1973, the Arab oil exporting nations announced their boycott, sending a chill through the ski industry. Automobiles were virtually the only way that skiers would travel. The old snow trains were long gone; buses were too inconvenient. If gasoline became tight, then the 1973/74 season could

Carlos Otis Stratton Mountain Clinic

It seemed that the logical person to talk to about the Clinic was Mary Beth Hand. "M.B." as she is called, was trained at St. Vincent's Hospital in New York and came to the Clinic when it first opened, and has been with it ever since. As the Clinic grew, Mary Beth's responsibilities grew with it and she has become a combination Head Nurse and a very pretty "Boss Lady." Here are some of her recollections:

"Back in 1971, I suddenly became aware that the foundation being built near the Base Lodge was going to be the realization of a dream of Philip Snyder. His efforts to build a clinic that would be called The Carlos Otis Clinic were finally coming true. A clinic that would provide injured skiers with emergency care very shortly after an accident—and most importantly—without driving many miles over winter roads to get that care.

Dr. Carlos Otis had cared for countless injured skiers, during Stratton's first years, at Grace Cottage Hospital in Townshend, and had endeared himself to all who came in contact with him. But it was time to have facilities on the Mountain and a major part of Phil's dream was to have the Clinic bear the name of "Townshend's Legendary Doctor." And to also have Dr. Otis serve as Medical Director—which he still does to this day.

"The doors opened January 2, 1972, with the best equipment and orthopedic care available. A unique system of doctor rotation had been worked out by Dr. Otis and a prominent Boston orthopedic surgeon, Dr. William MacAusland (who has just completed his term as President of the American Academy of Orthopedic Surgeons). Dr. MacAusland volunteered to recruit orthopedists for the new clinic and in exchange for donating their time they would receive lodging and skiing privileges for themselves and their families.

"In the past ten years the Clinic has treated over 8,400 patients. Skiers have managed to injure themselves going uphill and downhill; not to mention falling off the bannisters and off the barstools! The Clinic has been there to help even those unfortunate few with serious injuries. They can receive essential "stabilization" care followed by immediate transportation to a hospital in the Clinic's ambulance.

"General medical care is provided by Dr. Robert Homes on a year round basis. Not everyone is a skier; and the inevitable "bug" that surfaces several times a winter shows no sport preference and keeps Dr. Homes hopping.

"Dr. Otis, Phil Snyder, Casey Rowley, Dennie Davison, Gail Miller, Stephanie Wyley, Marykay Darby—a few of the many who have kept our Clinic running smoothly. I cannot finish my recollections without a thought for Helen Hart who helped me learn

be a complete bust.

Clifford moved promptly to obtain a gasoline allotment and to install tanks and pumps in Parking Lot 2. All publicity was centered around the message that every car arriving at Stratton would be assured of being able to fill up its tank before leaving—a promise that was carried out all the next season.

The 1973/74 season now got off to a shaky start with marginal snow conditions. Rain persisted through December and January; reliable natural snow did not begin to arrive until late February, by which time the season was two-thirds over. At the same time, gasoline was becoming very short everywhere, making it more and more difficult for skiers to find enough fuel to make the trip to Vermont. Total attendance for the season declined 34.5%.

The result was Stratton's poorest year since opening in 1961. Total revenues were only $2.2 million, and there was a big loss of $265,000.

Plans were quickly drawn to extend the snowmaking system to the summit. This would require a major new source of water and a second reservoir. A search was begun, and two alternatives were developed. One was the golf course lake. The second was to build a new pond which would tap Gulf Brook up on the West Hill. The golf course source was preferred by the contractor—Larchmont Engineering—but would require enormous pumps and over a mile of pipe through the golf course and chalet area just to bring the water to the base area. The Gulf Brook reservoir, on the other hand, would feed by gravity. Nevertheless, the decision went to the golf course lake; pumps and pipe were soon purchased; and engineering work began. It was anticipated that an Act 250 permit would soon be obtained and that the installation would be ready for the 1974/75 season.

"practical orthopedics" during the first two years. Helen is gone now, but I'll never forget her incredible ability to run her fingers along a lower leg, and with great certainty predict "that's a spiral tib-fib fracture!" Though just a "first Aider," she was correct ninety-nine percent of the time.

"From caring for an owl with a fractured wing (thanks, Dr. Love!), to patching up a "tray slider" on the bottom of the Suntanner—the Clinic has proven to be a wonderful asset to the Stratton community."

Clinic Day: Mary Beth Hand, Stephanie Wylie, Phil Snyder, Dr. Carlos Otis and David Clark during a 1980 fundraising.

Phil Snyder has retired as President of the Clinic board, but continues to serve as a Director. The present board consists of:

President James Tierney
Vice President and Treasurer William Simmer
Clerk Attorney Lawrin Crispe
Administrator Dr. Carlos Otis
Directors:
Dr. William MacAusland
Nelson Smith
Ski Patrol Liason
Casey Rowley
Philip Snyder
Don Tarinelli
Imre Cholnoky
Hugh Smith
Bob Hundt
Allan Fisher
Jerry Little

At the same time, negotiations were faltering with International Paper Realty Corp. Clifford had held a number of meetings with the new operating heads of IPR—Gordon Edwards and Jim Vanderwater (Don Foote and Bob Andrews having retired). They agreed to the installment sale of the Sun Bowl plus a mountain lease extension of 35 years. But, somehow, the deal would not gel. Edwards and Vanderwater seemed to be running into opposition at the parent company and apparently could not get the lease extension approved.

In September, they came back with a new counterproposal: IPR would develop the Sun Bowl alone and Stratton would get only the lease extension. This was just as unsatisfactory in 1974 as it had been in 1970. And so, at its September 14th meeting, the Stratton Board voted to terminate further negotiations to acquire additional lands in the Sun Bowl.

The Snowmaking Expansion Is Stalled

At the same meeting, it was necessary to postpone all action on extending snowmaking to the summit. They had run into problems with the Department of Water Resources, which opposed the golf course location as being too close to the Spray Irrigation site for the new sewage treatment plant. They would have to start all over again up on West Hill. The Company had been delayed a year.

At the 1974 annual stockholders' meeting in October, Luke Crispe announced his retirement from the Board. He was the first of the five original founding directors to resign. Luke has a passion for travel; he wanted to spend the coming years exploring some of the remote places of the world with his wife, Miriam, and he had already begun to turn over his Brattleboro law practice to his son, Lawrin. His colleagues were sad to lose his wise counsel—he had repeatedly steered the Company clear of trouble over the last fourteen years, and he would be missed.

A new director came onto the Board at this time: H. Rogers Bishop. One of the original stockholders and chalet owners at Stratton, Bishop brought the total number of directors back to eleven, with one vacancy.[10]

In November, the Board formally adopted the Gulf Brook reservoir site. Again, engineering studies were put in hand, so that work could begin promptly the following March. They already had $600,000 worth of pumps and pipes on hand for reconstruction of the snowmaking system, none of which could be used for a whole twelve months yet.

[10] The Directors in 1974 were: Frank V. Snyder, Harvey Clifford, E. Philip Snyder, Carlos G. Otis, Edward G. Janeway, Warren Hellman, John O. Morris, H. O. Smith, Nelson M. Smith, and Philip K. Allen.

Tink Smith was becoming more active in management again and volunteered to negotiate with Jim Carlaw (who headed up IP's Woodland Division) to obtain approval of the Gulf Brook reservoir site and also to see what progress could be made on renegotiating the Mountain lease.

By January, Smith had IP's offer to lease 33 acres to the Corporation for ten years at an annual rent of $1,650 per year. The Stratton Board accepted and immediately voted to go forward with the necessary Environmental and Water Resources permits to construct a five acre reservoir adjacent to Gulf Brook.

By January 1975, everyone was feeling much better. Christmas-New Year's 1974 had been a tremendous success, with revenues through January 3 up to $892,700—a full 131% above the previous year. All costs were running under budget. As usual, Clifford had a tight rein on overhead.

The lift privileges granted to the original bondholders were going to run out in a year; a three man committee (consisting of Bishop, Hellman and Tink Smith) was appointed to study what might be done to accommodate these investors. The committee came up with an offer to the bondholder to exchange his $1,000 bond for a $1,000 "pass credit" entitling him to exchange this for season passes through 1981. The Pass Credits were voted through at the next annual meeting.

In March, the remaining vacancy on the Board was filled by appointment of Fergus Smith. Tink Smith's son-in-law, Fergus had been quietly buying Stratton Corp. stock. The Smith family now owned almost 80,000 shares—about twice as much as the Snyders.

Tink Smith now let it be known that he again would like to be considered for the office of President. Snyder did not oppose him. This meant, of course, that Clifford had to go—a bitter pill, but, at the March Board Meeting, he stated for the record that he was leaving with no regrets and that he was proud of his accomplishments; he also announced his willingness to stay on through the coming summer in order to help with the transition.

Other management changes were approved at this time. One was the decision to hire Cal Conniff as Vice President and General Manager of Ski Operations; another was the appointment of David Meinertz as Marketing Director.

Conniff was Executive Director of the National Ski Areas Association at the time and had been General Manager at Mt. Tom in Holyoke, Mass. for a number of years before that. In May, he began looking for a home in Manchester but soon became discouraged—his family was unwilling to make the move to Vermont. So he withdrew in August, electing instead to stay on at NSAA, and Stratton started a new search for a General Manager.

Meinertz had arrived, meanwhile. A handsome ex-Marine first Lieutenant who had had a long term of duty in Vietnam; he was a bombshell thrown into the quiet Stratton community. Working day and night, he came up with an entirely new marketing plan by September and submitted it to the Board. For the first time, Stratton had a coherent and detailed marketing program to study. Two of Meinertz's ideas were immediately put in the works: a cross country center on the golf course and a skating pond near the Chapel. Unfortunately, though, Meinertz and Tink Smith disagreed on how the marketing department should operate, and by October, Meinertz was gone, leaving behind him, nevertheless, a model marketing plan.

The second executive search concluded in August, ended with the selection of Donald Tarinelli for the number two job in the Company. Although he had had no experience in the ski business, Tarinelli's business record was impressive. A graduate of Massachusetts Institute of Technology, he had worked for twenty years in the real estate construction business, building apartment houses and shopping centers all over New England. He was a strong Stratton booster, having owned a chalet there for years and having been a director of the Ski Education Foundation, as well as the co-founder (with Warren Hellman) of the Stratton Mountain School. He had just retired from the real estate business and was looking for a challenge somewhere in Vermont. It was a good fit.

The changeover took place at the 1975 annual meeting. It was Harvey Clifford's last appearance as an officer and director of the Company, and he left the Company in fine condition. It had been the best year in Stratton's history, with sales of $3.9 million and profits of $239,000. Borrowings had been reduced by $850,000 to $1.2 million, the lowest in many years.[11]

John Layman also resigned at this time. He was Clifford's close associate and went to Glen Ellen with Harvey and later to Big Sky in Montana.

Both Tink Smith and Don Tarinelli were installed in their new roles this day. They were both determined to bring an end to what they regarded as the stagnation of the Clifford years.[12] They would get Stratton moving again and would restore the vigor of the early years.

To do this, they had some things going for them besides their own enthusiasm and capacity for hard work: a superb plant, a first-rate staff, sound financial condition, and a Company whose environmental problems were pretty much behind it. There were problems ahead too: the lease on the Mountain was running out, and IP had shown little interest so far in extending it; operating expenses were on the rise, and "front-end costs" for roads, utilities, and environmental protection were steadily escalating. While this made it almost impossible for new competition to develop, it made expansion almost prohibitively expensive too.

Nevertheless, the watchword for the next six years would now be expansion: not just on the Mountain, but in the base area as well. Recognizing the immense underlying value of its real estate, both Smith and Tarinelli were convinced that the Corporation should be involved in its development, extending operations beyond skiing. They felt that, to be successful over the long run, Stratton should become both a winter and a summer recreational resort.

Meanwhile, Snyder, although still Chairman of the Board, no longer participated in management, as he had with Clifford. This was all right with him. Stratton was in safe hands, and he did not have time to give to its affairs as he had over the last fifteen years. His primary business responsibility continued to be Moore & Munger, Inc., which was rapidly expanding and requiring more of his energy. Beginning in 1976, his involvement at Stratton declined.

The Company Enters the Hotel Business

It was not long before the opportunity arose for the new management to urge the Company into new directions. Just before Christmas, 1976, the two owners of Stratton Mountain Inn, Pat Grant and William Lee, decided that it was time for them to put the Inn on the market. This holding represented far too large a percentage of their personal estates, they had concluded, so Pat called on Tarinelli and offered to sell to Stratton.

After getting clearance to negotiate, Tarinelli arrived at the January 10, 1976 Board meeting with an agreed-on price of $800,000, including the mortgage. He had taken the precaution of approaching SMI's mortgagee, Vermont National Bank, to find out how much the Bank would increase the mortgage if Stratton Corporation purchased and discovered that it could be raised to $700,000. Thus, the Inn could be purchased for only $100,000 cash. Leveraged in this way, he argued, there was no doubt that it would make good money for the Company. Also, he

[11] Although Clifford claimed that he was tired of skiing and almost never put his skis on anymore, he did have one secret ambition, which was to emulate his brother, John, who was Canada's most successful ski area entrepreneur. At this Stratton Annual Meeting, Harvey announced that he had just purchased Glen Ellen ski area. He was to sell it again three years later and then retire.

[12] Stratton's Board had consistently refused to approve of further expansion of ski facilities without a lease extension.

pointed out, the Inn did as much business in the summer as in the winter and so would help to even out the ups and downs in the Company's presently highly seasonal pattern of income.

Several directors nevertheless, opposed the purchase. Rogers Bishop, Warren Hellman, and Phil Snyder did not think this was the best use of the Company's money.

Tink Smith, on the other hand, was strongly behind the purchase, saying that, with Stratton Corp. operating the Inn, a high quality operation would be insured. Tarinelli favored the purchase, but only if the Company were to build a tennis center at the same time. He had been researching tennis centers and had concluded that this was an excellent amenity to attract summer visitors. A tennis center, he said, could be a profit center on its own merits, but it wouldn't be feasible to own an inn on the mountain without one, since the inns would be the primary beneficiaries. A cost study was then run, and a memorandum was submitted to the Board which advocated construction of a tennis center at a cost of $300,000. It would be operated by John Newcombe and could be completed for the coming summer season. The Board voted 9 to 2 (Hellman and Bishop opposed) to go forward with it.

By March, an ambitious capital spending program was put together; a new chair lift, completion of the golf course lake, the Tennis Center, and the first big investment in a joint venture with International Paper Realty Corp.

A New Joint Venture with International Paper

The IPR joint venture was an exciting new development. Tarinelli had been working on it for almost a year. During the summer of 1975, he had been retained as a real estate consultant. He had spotted a piece of land owned by IP which he thought would be ideal for joint development—a 38 acre tract just above the maintenance building and downhill from the Company's main drinking water reservoir. It was on-slope and would provide for "ski-in and ski-out" convenience for 76 condominium units; it could be served by the present sewage treatment plant; and it was close to the main base area.

He had now worked up a rough proposal and had run it by the new management at IP Realty: IP to transfer the land over to IPR, who would contribute it to the joint venture; Stratton Corp. to do all the rest; i.e. take care of the architecture, get state and town approvals; build the buildings, contribute the water and sewer connections; and sell the units. A 12% management and sales commission would go to Stratton, after which the profits would be split 50-50. Tarinelli was confident that Stratton would net $500,000 from the project. The people at IP Realty were interested, and the joint venture proposal was put in the hands of lawyers for preparation of legal documents.

By April 1976, operating figures for the previous ski season were finalized, and they were not encouraging. Record rainfall had reduced attendance in spite of the expanded snowmaking capability, and revenues were down. It looked like they were facing a loss in the first year under new management.

The die had been cast for rapid expansion, nevertheless. Tarinelli was advocating that the Company raise $6 million to finance development over the next few years. Three million dollars would come from a new subordinated bond issue and three million from additional bank borrowings. The bond idea was not yet acceptable to the Board, but it was obvious that some additional bank financing was going to be required. Tarinelli began negotiating with the bankers.

The location of the next chair lift had already been made. It had been decided long ago that no new lifts or trails would be built in the Sun Bowl until some sort of arrangement could be made with IPR on that base area, and so the next lift had to be built on the north face. The time was long overdue to take out the old T-bars. Chair Lift No. 7 would replace both of them, loading in the same spot as the lower T-bar and taking skiers up to a place where they could easily reach the North American lift. Bob Heron, designer of Stratton's first six lifts and now retired, was retained to draw up specifications. Requests for bids went out to all of the major U.S. manufacturers, and Borvig was selected. The new lift was unusual in one respect: although it would be operated as a double chair for the first few years, it would be built heavily enough to be easily converted to be a triple chair lift some time in the future. Design was completed in May; Act 250 approval was gotten; and construction began in June. Karl Bauer also reshaped and widened both Lower Tamarack and the old T-Bar Liftline, the latter of which was christened "Craig's Run" in honor of Craig Swart, who had just died.

Construction of the tennis courts had begun in early April, and the John Newcombe Tennis Center opened with eight outdoor and two indoor courts on schedule—a tribute to Tarinelli's construction skill.

The formal joint venture contract with IP Realty was drafted, reviewed, and executed, and the first nine Shatterack condominiums were begun. It was a busy summer.

While this construction was going on, a decision came in from the bankers. Stratton had requested a package consisting of $1.5 million long term and

$1.5 million revolving line of credit. The banks concluded that this amount was excessive, based on Stratton's performance of the past few years. They offered only $1.5 million long term and a $500,000 revolving credit, and recommended that Stratton proceed with its bond issue. This was not enough to complete projects already under construction.

A New Volunteer Fire Company

Over the years, there had been several serious fires on the Mountain. Louis Cabot's home had burned to the ground, apparently because of an untended fireplace fire; then the Hancocks' house had been seriously damaged, followed by the loss of Don Tarinelli's chalet. The Reichelms' beautiful home on West Hill had been totally consumed in thirty minutes, when their two-story indoor Christmas tree had ignited. The Bondville Fire Department was excellent and improving all the time, but, still, it was four miles away, and it took a while for a loaded fire truck to climb the Access Road.

In July, a group of chalet owners and employees formed the Stratton Mountain Fire Company, with John Plank as President. By the end of the summer, they had six full-time Mountain residents qualified in fire fighting techniques, with another 16 in training. Search was now instituted for a modern fire truck.

By October 1976, when Tarinelli stood up before the stockholders for his first Annual Meeting as General Manager, he had some good news and some bad news: the good news being that the Company was winding up its most ambitious summer program ever, with over $2 million in construction being completed; the bad news being that due to the rainiest winter in history to date the fiscal year had ended with a loss of $189,000—the second biggest in the Company's history.

At the director's annual meeting which followed, Tink Smith announced that he intended to remain on as President only so long as "necessary to get corporate functions moving smoothly again" (as Lawrin Crispe, clerk of the Corporation recorded it in the minutes). He promised that he would step down within a year to allow Tarinelli the top job, if all went well.

An Obstacle to Long Term Development Is Removed

The biggest obstacle for Stratton's long term development still remained, however. The lease from IP would expire in less than 10 years, which fact blocked the issuance of subordinated bonds and precluded any further development in the Sun Bowl. In order for the Company to proceed, the lease had to be dealt with. During his negotiations over this issue with IP, Tarinelli authored the concept which finally broke the log jam. He suggested that IP donate the land to a non-profit organization. IP showed interest, so Tarinelli approached Warren Hellman, who had taken over as the President of the U.S. Ski and Education Foundation, the organization which raises money for and operates the U.S. Ski Team.

Why not have IP donate the Stratton lease hold to the USSEF, which was the funding arm of the U.S. Ski Team, and they in turn lease the land to Stratton for 99 years—thus gaining its annual rent—and the Stratton Corporation would gain the long term lease hold it needed. Everybody would gain.

The idea was welcomed by IP's management, and final terms of the deal were put together in the last days of 1976. Stratton's stockholders met on January 20 to ratify the change, Rogers Bishop predicting to the assembled group that "with this lease extension, Stratton can now embark on long term development and hopefully secure long term financing."

To mark the occasion, IP donated a permanent trophy for amateur races to be held on the Mountain, and Vice President Wilford Lewis journeyed to Stratton to make the first award of prizes.

USSEF President Warren Hellman and IP Vice President Wilford Lewis with the perpetual trophy of the annual race at Stratton commemorating the IP donation of ski area terrain.

There was jubilation on the Mountain in that January and February of 1977. Even though there had been virtually no natural snow until mid-January, there was a new feeling of direction and accomplishment. The second Annual Winter Festival was directed by Jeff Dickson and, everyone agreed, was a great success, with parachute jumps, free style competitions, ski joring contests, and even classical music concerts, interspersed with the brauhaus entertainment of the Stratton Mountain Boys.

Previous to this transaction with IP, Warren Hellman had tendered his resignation as a Stratton Director in order to devote all efforts in guiding the U.S. Ski Team's destiny. He was to continue to be a Stratton skier, though, keeping his chalet and supporting the junior racing program and the Stratton Mountain School. Stratton had now lost another of its best directors, a man who had done much for the Company in his short time on the board.[13]

A New Long Range Plan

The agreement with IP then set the stage for a new long range plan and Zane Yost, a Bridgeport, Connecticut architect and planner, was engaged. Working together, Tarinelli and Yost focused in two areas: the main base and the Sun Bowl. Their recommendation was that the main base area—with its concentrated development of facilities—continue to be the primary commercial village. Instead of building a village around the Chapel, as had been originally planned, they agreed with Goubert's concept of placing it on the ski slopes, but further east and directly up hill from Lift Line Lodge and Birkenhaus. To accommodate it, the Access Road would be moved downhill about 100 feet. The Village would have no architectural connection with the Base Lodge, however, which would remain the center for day skiers.

In the Sun Bowl, the planning work identified terrain which was suitable for the second golf course, and which was suitable for residential or lodging. None of this was offered as a final plan, it being Tarinelli's dictum that planning is a process, and that long range plans should give direction and logic for orderly growth rather than being determinate and finite.

Expansion of the Base Lodge

Plans were now being made for expansion of the Base Lodge. Much thought was going into a study of how additional seating could be provided without making the crowding even worse. The building had originally been designed to seat 800, but a count of chairs now revealed that there were only 700 chairs. The best way to go—everyone agreed—was to convert the present ski shop and ski rental into additional cafeteria, to remove all other non-restaurant functions from the building, and to increase seating capacity to over 1,000. This would have the added advantage of avoiding the necessity of building a new kitchen and storage area elsewhere. It also meant that a new ski shop building would have to be erected. At the same time, the Ski School desperately needed a new nursery and cub school building, while facilities were needed for ticket sales and ski weekers reception. Sandy McIlvaine was retained again to put all these rough ideas together.

In February, it was decided that, if a new ski shop building was going to have to be built, the Company should take over the retail and rental operations. Peter Pringham and Charlie Sonnenfeld had had this franchise from the very beginning at Stratton. They had done a fine job, and it was difficult to bring the business relationship with these old friends to a close. Both Pringham and Sonnenfeld decided to retire. The Norse House name was thereupon assigned to a group of former employees who, headed up by Harry Robinson, planned to erect a new building in Bondville and to carry on the business.

Another New Chair Lift and Hurricane Belle

Capital spending that summer of 1977 was limited to construction of Lift No. 8, the "Grizzly" lift, as it was to be generally known, one new trail, the "Bear Bottom", snowmaking under Lift No. 7, and the final touches on the Golf Course Lake.

There had never been an easy way back to the summit for those skiers coming over from Sun Bowl or for those who just skied down Black Bear or Polar Bear. The Grizzly lift would solve that. The loading point was placed at the foot of the Polar Bear runout, with unloading on the summit, near the beginning of Upper Tamarack Trail. The lift would be 4,800 feet long on a vertical of 1,200 feet and with a capacity of 1,200 skiers per hour. Once again, Borvig was the contractor.

Work was proceeding smoothly, when in August, catastrophe struck in the form of Hurricane Belle. This strange storm charged ashore at the mouth of the Connecticut River and passed directly over Stratton Mountain, right on the heels of a two day northeast storm that had filled brooks and streams with six inches of rainfall.

Belle added another eight inches in the short period of six hours. The streams simply could not take this sudden influx. Flooding was widespread, and heavy damage resulted. In Bondville, a two hundred yard section of Route 30 was destroyed by the rampaging Winhall River. A car stalled on the Bondville Bridge, and the driver barely was able to reach safety before the waters swept it away downstream. In Jamaica, the damage was almost as bad. Two bulldozers belonging to Chancey Smith had been

[13] Some time later, Hellman negotiated the purchase of Aspen Ski Corporation by Twentieth Century Fox.

parked behind his house, which bordered on Ball Mt. Brook. Within a few minutes, the water had risen over the banks, and the bulldozers disappeared. The smaller of the two was last seen rolling end-over-end down the rampaging brook, while the larger one, a Caterpiller, was buried under tons of rock and gravel.

On the Mountain there were washouts everywhere. Three golf course greens were totally destroyed; almost every culvert, road, and driveway was knocked out. There was erosion on the trails, too, but surprisingly nowhere near as much as was at first anticipated—thanks to the heavy growth of deeply rooted grasses and the deep water bars. Curiously, the greatest damage was wrought by Kidder Brook over in the Sun Bowl. With the exception of the old "Mountain Road," Kidder Brook ran through unbroken forest for its whole length, and yet there the devastation was the greatest.

It was a strange storm. When all the reports were in, Jamaica, Bondville, and Stratton Mountain had suffered the most severe damage. Neither Bromley nor Mt. Snow nor the towns near them had anywhere near the same extent of losses.

The rest of August and September were spent in cleaning up the mess. When the stockholders arrived for their usual annual meeting on the first Saturday in October, there was little to show that a major hurricane had struck six weeks earlier.

The auditor's report for fiscal 1977 revealed that a profit of $20,000 had been earned on a turn-over of $4.9 million. At the annual meeting, Tink Smith stepped down as President, becoming co-Chairman along with Snyder, his farewell comments receiving a standing ovation from the stockholders. Tarinelli now assumed the title of President and Chief Executive Officer.

At the meeting, it was reported, among other things, that the Stratton Mountain School was flourishing in its new home in the old Hotel Tyrol. Seven graduates of the School were now members of the U.S. Ski Team squad, and one of them, fifteen year old Heidi Preuss, had just been placed on the A team for the coming season. There were now 60 students at the School, which was under the direction of headmaster Donald Burke.

In spite of the visit of Hurricane Belle, work had proceeded on the Grizzly chair lift, and it opened on schedule December 8. The conversion of Lift No. 7 from double to triple was accomplished at the same time, which meant that the uphill capacity had been increased by an astonishing 21% in one summer.

Another Record Year

The 1977/1978 season which followed was one of the best. One hundred ninety inches of natural snow fell, with a miniscule 6 inches of rain—a better record than any season for the last decade. The ski area operated for 135 days, averaging 1,789 skiers per day—an astounding 26% over the previous season. Total revenue for the fiscal year soared to $7.3 million; and when all the results were in, it was found that they produced a record profit of $310,-000, or a little less than 5% of sales.

At the Federation Internationale de Ski annual meeting in the previous summer, Stratton had been selected as one of the two U.S. sites for a World Cup Race in early March, 1978. There were to be both giant and special slaloms for men and women—four races in all—and the best amateur racers in the world would attend. North American trail was selected for the giant slalom, and Slalom Glade for the special. A new starting area was prepared on the Glade for the women, and numerous other preparations put in hand, including new starting and finish buildings, TV cable towers, a new scoreboard, and the like. One of the more imaginative structures was an ice sculpture fashioned at the ski school meeting place by the ski school instructors, led by Kasi Lindlebaur. In the center was a ten foot high icy replica of the famous Evian World Cup, around each side of which were placed 30-foot long ice-covered "bobsled" runs for children (and some adults too) to slide down. The final production was a work of art.

For a week before the races, North American and Slalom Glade were closed to the public, while Pat Williams' snowmaking crew and Donny Davison's grooming crew manicured the runs to perfection. It was necessary that they now have the right depth and density to stand up under the pounding. A racing organization, which numbered close to 450 persons—most of them volunteers—was assembled by Bob Hardy. When the first day of the races arrived, the weather cooperated. Several thousand spectators lined the courses to watch both of the Mahre twins win. Phil took the Giant Slalom, while, in the special slalom, his brother, Steve, defeated the odds-on favorite Ingmar Stenmark of Sweden. After so many years of conducting races, Stratton's devoted Ski Education supporters showed how to do it: each of the two women's special slalom runs—with over 50 competitors taking part—was completed in just over 30 minutes.

After the prizes had been awarded, and the cheering crowds had gone home; Stratton received the best accolade of all, when FIS technical delegate, Luc Dubois, wrote in his official report that the World Cup at Stratton was "by far the best race ever conducted in North America."

The ski area closed a month later on April 9, after what had been the most successful season in its history. Not only had Stratton received excellent publicity from the World Cup Race (including nationwide airing on the CBS Sports Spectacular), but, more importantly, the Company was now in better financial condition than it had been for two years. Over $1 million in bonds had now been sold; long term debt had been reduced to $1.6 million, and the total cash position exceeded $1.6 million, most of it in CDs. The stage was now set for the Base Lodge expansion.

Another Summer of Construction

McIlvaine's plans provided for three new buildings, each smaller in scale than the original Base Lodge, and each more or less connected. The nursery and cub school would front on the ski slope and would be fireproof. Downhill from it would be a small plaza surrounded by the ski shop and ski reception centers, each connected by a long, covered overpass, under which arriving skiers could walk to and from the parking lots. A small clock tower would set off the whole complex, architecturally.

A second project was initiated: a 32-room annex to the Stratton Mountain Inn. This would provide really nice suites on the main floor with two large "Breakout" meeting rooms in the basement/ground floor.

The Shatterack condominiums had sold like hot cakes the previous winter, and 25 more units were now started. Winding up the list of projects: steps were begun to move the maintenance building. IP Realty insisted on this as a condition of going forward with the joint venture and not without reason. The maintenance building bordered right on the edge of Shatterack and was an unattractive operation to have next door, what with snow cats running night and day and heavy equipment visibly parked in rows outside.

Taken together, it was the largest construction program yet attempted by the Company. Nearly $3.5 million was budgeted. It was hoped that bond sales would sell out and provide most of the necessary funds.

At the Annual Meeting in October, 1978, two new directors were voted in: Ellen McCormick and Clarence Michalis. Mrs. McCormick was a South Londonderry resident and an enthusiastic skier who would, it was hoped, bring a more local viewpoint to the Board. Michalis had recently retired as Vice President of Administration at Bristol Myers. A banker by training, his experience would be most helpful in watching over the financial affairs of the Company. To this end, an Audit Committee, to be chaired by Michalis, was now formed to keep tabs on the operation of the Company's Accounting Department.

In his report to stockholders at this annual meeting, Tarinelli pointed out that real estate sales had exceeded $500,000 for the first time in history, with a gross profit of $140,000—much of which was from sales of Shatterack condominiums. The stockholders were delighted to learn that the program had succeeded.

An Optimistic Outlook

Affairs were looking good during that Autumn of 1978. The base area extension was almost complete, and it was very handsome. The combination of varying roof lines and facades added enormously to the visual impact as visitors drove up the Access Road. The eighth chair lift—Grizzly—had run without a flaw the previous season. Most important of all, Stratton's staff of department heads were all veterans who knew their business and who were among the best in the entire industry.[14] Management was in good hands.

To the stockholders who gathered for the traditional lunch at Stratton Mt. Inn after the meeting, it appeared that Stratton had done it again: another successful expansion had been accomplished, and the Company seemed poised on the threshhold of a triumphant new era.

Some Bad News

Some bad news was already known. The bond issue had not come near selling out and was now some million dollars short of original projections. The cost of filing an extension was thought to be too high, and the issue was allowed to lapse. On the heels of this, overruns in last summer's construction programs were turning out to be larger than had been indicated last fall.

As usual, the Board delayed making any decisions as to the 1979 summer program until the results of the current ski season were in hand during March. The news presented at that time was not all that good. Skier visits were 20,000 below budget. Receipts were sharply down—$265,000 less than at the same date a year ago.

[14] Gary Plante was Vice President and Controller; Ralph Rawson—Vice President in charge of construction and maintenance; Tex Laidlaw—Assistant to the President. Karl Bauer was in charge of lifts and trails; Donny Davison—snow grooming; Pat Williams—snowmaking; Jeff Dickson—marketing; Mary Fraser—ski shop; Peter Hand—food and beverage; Emo Henrich—director of skiing; Jack Dudley—real estate; Casey Rowley—ski patrol and golf course; and Lester Williams—equipment operations and maintenance.

The year-end figures, which were available to the Board in late August, were not as bad as had been anticipated in March. Tarinelli's company plan had called for an attendance figure which would equal the previous year. Actually, attendance had fallen short by almost 20%, because of weather, but, even so, ski operating income had equalled 1978 because of higher prices, while real estate sales had actually doubled to over $1 million.

A Major Purchase

In September 1979, Stig Albertsson approached Tarinelli with an offer to sell Big Bromley to Stratton. Albertsson owned all of the outstanding preferred stock and 93% of the common. He had decided that smaller ski resorts were going to have a hard time surviving in the coming years. His reasons: the skiing market was showing definite signs of leveling out or even declining; ski area operating expenses were climbing with no sign that this trend would reverse. He had tried to make Bromley a big resort by offering to purchase control of nearby Okemo Mountain but had been defeated in his bid. Since he had been unable to purchase another resort of like size, he had concluded that he would have to sell to one of his bigger neighbors. There were three obvious possibilities: Killington, Sugarbush, or Stratton. He preferred to sell to Stratton, and so his first approach was there.

Tarinelli realized that the timing was not very good, but he recommended the purchase to the Board on the theory that, if Stratton didn't buy Bromley, then a Killington or Sugarbush would; and Stratton would be hurt in the process. Albertsson's price and terms were very fair, he believed, (both Smith and Snyder agreed): $2,389,000, with Stratton taking over Bromley's $2.4 million debt. It meant that Stratton would now be doubling its own debt to over $7 million. There were some plusses: Bromley offered warm side skiing (which Stratton lacked) and had five good chairlifts, three alpine slides, and excellent management. The Board voted unanimously for the purchase, and the stockholders ratified it by a large margin.

The news created a big stir down in the valley. The immediate reaction was one of universal relief: if Bromley had to be sold, it was far better that Stratton get it than that some outsiders, like Killington, move into the area, said townspeople.

Tarinelli now reassured Bromley's employees by saying that there would be no changes. He planned to spend much time there, familiarizing himself with the operation. Albertsson, meanwhile, retired from active management but joined Stratton's Board of Directors and Executive Committee. He knew he was leaving behind a strong, lean staff, with John Cueman as General Manager; Frank Johnson, Mountain Manager; Jim Marsh in charge of snowmaking; Dan O'Connor, Marketing Manager; Peter Mutz, food and beverage manager; and Ed Trudel, Ski School director.

Another Move Is Announced in 1979

Right on the heels of the Bromley purchase came another major announcement in December. Tarinelli had managed to negotiate a whole new joint venture agreement with IP Realty in which each company would share profits fifty-fifty and in which each would put in its development land. For Stratton, this was only about 56 acres, while for IPR, it was all of the Sun Bowl base area—or about 700 acres. The last obstacle to development of the Sun Bowl had been removed.

Once again, Stratton's people went into a new season charged up with enthusiasm and confidence in the future. All barriers had now been cleared away by Tarinelli's leadership, and they were ready to embark on the long-planned and hoped-for development of the east face of the Mountain.

Serious Problems Develop

What actually happened was disaster. Once again, natural snow was insignificant in November, December, and January, with skiing limited to snow making areas. Attendance was sparse. By the end of the Christmas/New Year's holiday, Stratton's total attendance was 23,000 compared with 53,000 in a normal year. Bromley suffered the same loss of patronage for the same reasons, and interest rates were continuing their ominous climb. It was rapidly becoming clear that this was a very bad time to have such a heavy debt burdening the Company.

By early February, 1979, the outlook was becoming gloomy. Treasurer Plante was predicting that if interest rates continued to remain high, the Company would not make it through the summer without at least $2 million of new capital just to meet operating requirements. If that new money did not come in, he said, the book value of the Company's stock would be down to $2 a share in June, and, by September, it would be zero.

At that point, Tarinelli felt that the additional funds could be raised by going to the banks. However, after studying the situation, Stratton's bankers said that, while they would come up with some new money, a large infusion of new equity was needed at the same time, i.e. a million in new stock for a million in additional bank financing.

For the first time in a long while, Stratton was up

against a stone wall. The Board immediately established an *ad hoc* Capital Committee to explore various avenues of raising new funds.

Affairs did not improve in February, and by the end of the month, the vista beyond the stone wall was looking more like a precipice.

Sitting in his Moore & Munger office one day in February, he reviewed the situation with the M&M Treasurer, David Rosow, concluding with the prediction that Stratton Corporation would be on the blocks by midsummer.

"You know, Dave," he said, "whoever buys that Company is going to get some terrific long term assets if they are willing to wait a few years." Snyder then asked him to attend a meeting of the *ad hoc* committee scheduled for the next day at the Moore & Munger offices. Perhaps, Snyder said, Rosow could offer some help.

Rosow agreed, and the conversation returned to Moore & Munger matters.

The two men had formed a close-knit team. Rosow had joined Moore & Munger in 1974 as Snyder's assistant, after having been in the securities business for a time and having served as a deck officer on the aircraft carrier "Forrestal" during the Vietnam war. Together, they had negotiated and concluded a successful merger two years before with the Chas. J. Wood Petroleum Co. Since then, Moore & Munger, Inc. had grown rapidly and had already passed $100 million in sales with a fine return on equity. Along with the third Director, S. T. "Pete" Van Esselstyn, they were now planning to break $200 million in sales by 1982 and were staffing up to make further expansion possible.[15]

At the meeting[16] Rosow listened to the discussion of various plans and to Snyder's comments that the options presented were nothing but bandaids. Tarinelli reported that he would be required to reduce Stratton's operations to the bone, laying off some 200 people, in order to open the next November. Finally, Rosow asked a question out loud but to no one in particular,

"What would Stratton pay for an equity infusion of $3-4 million?"

Michalis and Bishop responded simultaneously, "Control, of course, but who would possibly come up with that kind of cash?"

Rosow then suggested that M&M might make such an investment, under the proper terms.

Snyder was thunderstruck. The idea simply had not occurred to him. For nearly twenty years, he had tried to keep Stratton's and Moore & Munger's affairs separate and distinct. He immediately voiced an objection, saying,

"You know, there's no way that that purchase would meet the criteria we have set up at Moore & Munger for acquisitions."

He then added, "There's no way I can be a part of it, and you know it. I can't even say whether I think it's a good deal for Moore & Munger or not."

Rosow then told Snyder that he and Van had discussed the idea very early that morning. Van had agreed with the analysis that Rosow had made, and both realized that this purchase would have to be put together without any consultation with Snyder. The meeting adjourned with Rosow agreeing to attend a regular Stratton Board meeting the next day and (after review with "Van" again) perhaps to make a firm offer.

After the Stratton contingent departed, Snyder, Van Esselstyn and Rosow met. Snyder was asked if he had any philosophical problems with the deal to which he replied, "No." He then left the room and began his drive to Vermont.

The offer was presented to Stratton's Board on March 1.[17]

Tink Smith did not attend that March 1 meeting. He was in Florida, but he had been in touch with Fergus Smith by phone. Neither of them were convinced that the Company was in as serious condition as were the other directors. Janeway, Michalis, and Bishop were all in favor of the proposal. At the meeting, Tarinelli stated for the record that, as a businessman, he felt that the proposal represented a superb solution to the difficult problems facing the Corporation in the immediate future.

Snyder left the meeting, while the remaining directors discussed the situation. Fergus Smith suggested that the Company should explore other alternatives before resorting to sale of company stock, and he suggested borrowing additional funds from First National Bank of Boston. Tarinelli disagreed, stating that one of the principal reasons for the Company's position at the present time was the tremendous interest expense brought about by the great debt load and high interest rates (as well as poor weather). After further discussion, it was decided to have a special Board meeting a week later

[15] Moore & Munger's employees knew that this was probably the largest privately owned company in the U.S., all of whose stock was owned by the employees themselves. With a growth rate of 100% a year over the last four years, Moore & Munger was also one of the fastest growing medium-sized companies in the country at the time.

[16] Attending were: Frank & Phil Snyder, Tarinelli, Janeway, Michalis, Bishop and Gary Plante.

[17] The Board had just set up honorary directorships for retiring directors and had appointed Luke Crispe as the first Honorary Director: John Morris and Phil Allen now announced that they wished to join Luke on the sidelines.

with Tink Smith present to vote on the proposition.

The next week was hectic, both at Moore & Munger and Stratton. Tarinelli and Rosow had agreed to a purchase price of $3,750,000 for 750,000 shares (80% of the equity), plus a loan to Stratton, "from time to time," of another $1 million working capital.

Tink Smith had announced that he did not want to be a small minority stockholder. He still did not think the Company was in such serious trouble that it would have to be sold if no new equity was forthcoming. He would, therefore, agree to the sale only if his own and his family's stock was exchanged for developable base area land appraised at a value equal to the offer of Moore & Munger. This was accomplished by transferring the eleven acres of base area land designated in the Yost Plan as the Village for the shares of "family" stock. Stratton also agreed to buy shares from other shareholders at $5 per share. In total, some 92,000 shares, including the Smith's, were tendered—some 38% of all the outstanding stock.

On March 8, the special board meeting took place, and the directors unanimously accepted the offer (Snyder not being present). A month later, the stockholders ratified the sale, and Stratton became a subsidiary of Moore & Munger, Inc. Two new directors were elected: Pete Van Esselstyn and David Rosow.

Immediately after the closing, Rosow attended the first staff meeting to reassure the employees that there would be no immediate changes. Although Stratton was now a subsidiary of Moore & Munger, it was intended that it should continue to operate independently with its own Board making fiscal and policy decisions and management reporting through Tarinelli to Rosow and thence to Snyder. Nevertheless, Rosow carefully pointed out, Stratton must stand on its own feet, must control its costs, and must not expect to be supported by Moore & Munger at every turn.

Although it had been promised that no changes would occur, Tarinelli had already brought two Bromley men over to Stratton; John Cueman was deeply involved in reorganizing certain departments, and Dan O'Connor had come to take over sales and promotion, David Clark having left the Company. On July 26, Cueman was named Executive Vice President, and Emo Henrich and Casey Rowley were appointed Vice Presidents. Frank Johnson was elected Vice President and General Manager of Bromley. After ten years as Bromley's Ski School Director, Ed Trudel now decided he would rather sell real estate in Vail, Colorado. Paul Johnson was thereupon appointed the new Director of the Bromley Ski School.

The infusion of new capital enabled the Company immediately to reduce short and long term debt, and a new revolving credit of $6 million was arranged. Disaster had been averted and passed, but it still had to be proven that the Company could be profitable over the long haul in a period of very high interest rates, rapid inflation, and rising operating costs.

Again the make-up of the Board changed, Ellen McCormick had just moved to Connecticut, and she now resigned, along with Fergus Smith, who was no longer a stockholder. Tink Smith remained a director—in recognition of his long service—and Louis Cabot and Bill Sneath were elected to the Board.[18]

The summer capital program for 1980 was $1,250,000. Bromley was already undergoing a major face-lift brought about by the relocation and rebuilding of Route 11 by the State Highway Department. The Company was obligated to contribute $250,000 for its share of these construction costs. The Bromley Ski Shop was renovated, and, late in the Fall, when the Cracker Barrel Ski Shop in Rawsonville became available, Stratton took a lease on it. Snowmaking was installed on the upper Tamarack and Lower Grizzly. Then the new Kidder Brook lift line was cut and foundations poured. The Borvig lift would be 6,500 feet long on a vertical of over 1,500 feet—by far the largest lift on the mountain. The Base Lodge area was cleaned up, a clock tower added, and asphalt put down. The Styles Brook construction program got underway, and 15 units were built and eventually sold.

Everyone now expected the 1980/1 ski season to be a big improvement over the previous two years, but Mother Nature was not cooperating. Temperatures on Christmas Day stayed below −20 °F; the wind chill temperature at the summit was −85 °F. New Year's weekend was bitter cold. Then, in February, the warm weather that had been plaguing Colorado reached Vermont, bringing temperatures up into the 70s. At season's end, attendance at the two areas showed improvement over 1979/80, but once again, sharply increased operating and interest costs had wiped out any chance for making a profit on skiing. Nevertheless, healthy real estate sales, a lower tax rate, and several extraordinary items allowed the Company to show a record profit of $667,400, although, without the M&M capital infusion, Stratton would have lost several hundred thousand dollars.

[18] Both had had extensive business experience, Louis Cabot as Chairman of Cabot Corporation and Bill Sneath as Chairman of Union Carbide.

A Condo Hotel and a Change in Management

During the winter, Tarinelli had been readying plans for a new condominium hotel in the base area. Condo-hotels were a rather new concept; the investor purchases one or more rooms in the hotel, pays his share of expenses and receives the tax benefits of ownership (including depreciation) and a share of the income. His use of the room is restricted—usually to two weeks a year.

The Klett Organization of Pennsylvania was retained to draft plans for a 90-unit hotel in the Village area. A model was prepared and a prospectus filed with SEC. Widespread interest was developed among Stratton skiers. However, the contractor's bid in late April 1981, was 50% greater than originally anticipated. It appeared at that time that an investment in the condo hotel would not be feasible.

Frank Snyder, meanwhile, retired as Moore & Munger's President, and David Rosow replaced him in the top job. Unfortunately, Rosow and Tarinelli had increasing trouble communicating with each other and could not agree on corporate policy. Besides, each had very different personalities and probably fundamentally different ideas on how the area should be expanded. Anyway, the end came quickly. In June, 1981, Tarinelli was offered a limited role as a consultant to finalize the Sun Bowl development plan and was requested to resign as President. He declined and was abruptly discharged. Stig Albertsson was hired to pilot the Company.

The change rocked the Company; fears were expressed among some of the employees. Albertsson sought to assure the staff by announcing that no major changes would occur.

During that same winter and spring period, Tarinelli and Rosow completed negotiations with IP Realty for the bulk sale of the Sun Bowl property—the same transaction that Clifford had come so close to consummating six years earlier. The final details were pinned down in a 3 AM phone call with the Chairman of IPR, Rosow negotiating from his hotel room in Taiwan, after a 14-hour airplane trip. The terms were $4,750,000 with $1,500,000 down and the balance payable in installments. The last barrier had been cleared for controlled development of the Mountain.

Meanwhile, all spring long, Bret Hall, Rosow's assistant, had been spending time making computer runs to determine at what point the condo hotel would be feasible, and, in July, he came up with the recommendation that a minimum of 196 units be constructed. Architect Klett expanded his plans; and, when this was accomplished, new bids were sought. These were studied during July; the decision was made to go forward if bank financing and an Act 250 permit could be obtained. Either the project had to start on September 1 or be delayed until spring 1982. The Act 250 permit required another hearing, which was held on August 27, and the permit was granted on the same day. Bank financing could not be put together so quickly, however, and the project was deferred until spring of 1982. The Village would have to wait another six months.

Conclusion

December 22, 1981, marks the twentieth anniversary of the opening of this beautiful mountain resort called Stratton.

Twenty years are only a brief interlude when measured against the 372 years that have passed since Samuel de Champlain first looked across the waters of the lake that was to bear his name, and saw the mountains of Vermont. And compared to the long years of struggle for the communities surrounding Stratton Mountain, a period of twenty years perhaps has little significance. But to those who created this new Stratton the years from 1961 to 1981 represent a long time. It is actually a generation of hard work and endeavor by individuals who placed little value on their time in order to build something that others might enjoy. The same is true for Stratton's recently adopted sister, Bromley, who was born forty-four years ago. In the process, those operations (which were truly hobbies) have now been overtaken by events and are full-fledged Corporations. This phenomenon has been typical of the ski industry. Capital today is expensive; time more so.

Faceless corporations have taken over to control many ski areas—but not at Stratton. Moore & Munger is carrying on the legacy left us by Fred Pabst, Frank Snyder, Tink Smith and Ed Janeway—the legacy which is, first of all, an example of vision and courage and, secondly, the creation of two institutions which provide recreation for thousands and 850 jobs.

Will that continue? Certainly, because each of these three companies have traditions and methods of doing business which makes them quality leaders in their fields. Stratton is the junior in this group, but it has shown tremendous spirit over the years. It has done many great things with very little capital. Perhaps, in the coming years, the Stratton dream will mature and, at long last, we will see the East's finest winter and summer resort completed on the flanks of Stratton Mountain.

In the Beginning...

These scenes, taken from original 16mm film shot by Frank Snyder, trace the early stages of Stratton's development. Stratton's magnificent Base Lodge (top left) was under construction in late 1960. Welding of steel support beams was done in the bitter cold of December. Bob Wright, Tink Smith and Elmer Argast (row one, third photo from top) stand at the Base Lodge site in the Autumn of 1960 surveying the terrain.

Gene Gillis and Emo Henrich (bottom, center row) pause from their difficult tasks of organizing their respective operations. It was Gillis who designed nearly all of the North Face trails. Jesse Snyder (second from top, center row) rests on logs cut by Lester Williams and Wally Roberts at the top of Tyrolienne slope, in the fall of 1960. Seeding and haying the trails was done by Karl Bauer's young crew.

In October, 1960, some 200 tons of material, including massive lift towers, were flown up the mountain by helicopter—a ski industry first. All hands worked long and hard to meet the opening day schedule. Concrete was poured for the loading terminal of North American lift in late November (second from top, right row). The bull-wheel for this lift is shown being assembled (top right).

Then, in the Spring of 1961, members of the Vermont Legislature were invited to the Stratton Corporation offices, and to see the budding ski area (bottom left).

Life on the Mountain

MIDDLEBROOK
BLACK BEAR
GRIZZLY BEAR
POLAR BEAR

LIFTLINE LODGE

Stratton
Stratton

NASTAR
Junior NASTAR
NASTAR

Ski School
Meeting
Place
Stratton

stratton
WORLD CUP 78

K2
PHIL-RACE
USA
DESCENTE

Stratton Mtn. Boys

107

CUTRITE

Quarter Mile
Road

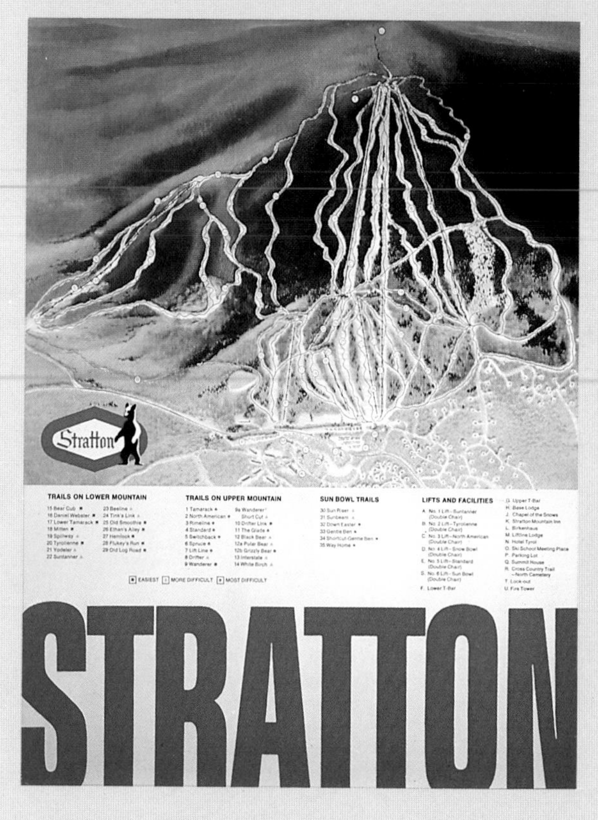

From the Archives...

Over the years, posters played their role in promoting the ski area. Clockwise, from the top left, is apparently Stratton's first poster, most probably from 1962; then 1965, 1968, 1969, 1970, and 1967.

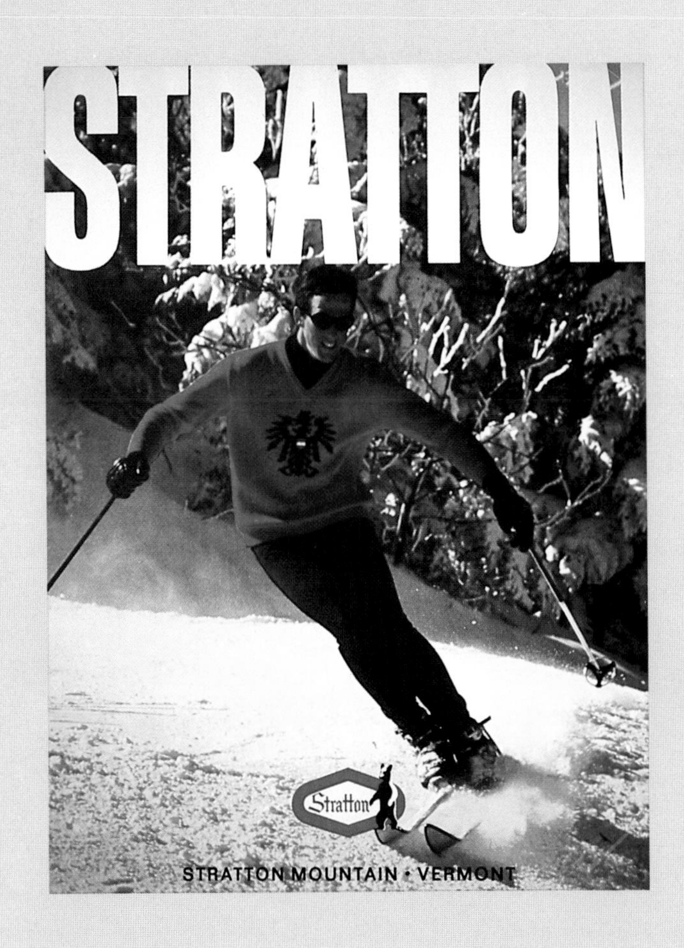
STRATTON
Stratton
STRATTON MOUNTAIN • VERMONT

STRATTON
STRATTON MOUNTAIN·VERMONT

STRATTON
VACATIONS
STRATTON MOUNTAIN·VERMONT

In the 1970's new shapes and sizes were in vogue: clockwise are posters from 1972, 1973, and 1975.

Stratton Profiles

Stig Albertsson

Stig Albertsson, a native of Sweden, became a resident of Manchester, Vermont, just ten years ago when he bought Bromley from Fred Pabst. Bromley, at that time, was not in the best of financial shape and Stig set to work to put the area back on its feet. Within a few years, Bromley once again held a prominent place in the ski industry.

In 1975, Albertsson began to investigate the possibility of bringing in the German manufactured Alpine Slide to America. By 1976 the first slide was installed at Bromley and Albertsson had the rights to the distributorship for the North American continent. This was a new venture requiring a lot of time and attention. Albertsson then decided to sell Bromley, and Stratton decided to buy. The final negotiations took place in June 1979. It was quite a surprise to the whole area, and the feelings were mixed. Mainly due to the fact that neither area wanted to lose its particular identity because of this take-over.

But the story wasn't finished—on June 12, 1981, Albertsson was elected President of Stratton Corporation. It was an announcement, in a series of announcements, that topped them all. With a somewhat ironic twist, Albertsson was returning to take over, not only his old ski area but also to be chief executive of what was once his major competition in the area.

There was much speculation about what was going to happen, but when asked, Albertsson replied:

> "I have no plans to make any great changes at this time; I think we need to look around and try to make improvements that will lead to savings and even more efficient operation." (Stratton Magazine/Fall 1981)

When you first meet Stig Albertsson, you are impressed by his quiet intelligence and calm manner. It almost conceals, what you already know about him—and that is his proven ability and determination to keep a business running smoothly and in good financial order.

Karl Bauer

There have been many times in the past twenty years when the only passable skiing in the East was here on the north face of Stratton Mountain. Eastern weather, being what it is, can destroy a ski slope in a matter of hours. To keep these slopes in condition takes a special group of men dedicated to their jobs and willing to face the adversity of Vermont's winter weather.

Since the inception of Stratton over 20 years ago, the leader of this rugged group of individuals has been Karl Bauer. A man perfectly suited to his job. Karl is in a word, tough. Both physically and mentally, Karl has driven his men over the years to achieve what is considered a "state-of-the-art" in slope and lift maintenance.

Karl came to Stratton from Germany by way of Mt. Snow, Okemo, and Killington ski areas. He was born in the village of Immenstadt in the province of Bavaria. As a youth he worked the long hours of a family farm, from sunup (where breakfast was served in the fields long after the day's work had begun) to sundown. It was this early life that forged Karl into the man that he is today. After some time at Killington, where he helped install their first chairlift, Karl met Frank Snyder. In 1960 Karl was hired by Frank and given the task of working with Gene Gillis, who was laying out trails and preparing for the installation of lifts.

A monumental task faced Karl and his men. In order to meet the time schedule for the opening of Stratton, the clearing of ski trails had to be done at the rate of an acre a day. In addition, the construction of the foundations for lift towers had to be completed and ready for the airlifting of the towers by helicopter. Karl took himself and his men to the limits, working ten hour days and solving the problems as they presented themselves. Somehow they managed to put it all together. As planned, three lifts were inspected and declared ready for Stratton's first skiers to use that Christmas week of 1961.

Karl retired in the spring of 1981. Twenty years have gone by and the mountain's record of excellence in trail and lift management stands as a monument to Karl's hard work and efficiency. Many times when other areas could barely offer any skiing at all, Stratton has been able to open its slopes because of the work of the trail maintenance crews that Karl directed. He has not been an easy man to work for, as many will tell you, but he believed in excellence and for this he earned the respect of all.

Irene Benson

For the majority of corporations in this country, the unknown and unsung heroine of the operation is the executive secretary whose duty it is to keep the boss' life simple so that he can concentrate on making those all important major decisions. In other words, she makes many of the small decisions in the day to day operation and performs countless thankless tasks.

For the first ten years of Stratton's existence when the ultimate success of the area depended on sound management and cooperation between the management team, it was Irene Benson who maintained the front office and organized the work of Tink Smith, Frank Snyder and general manager, Elmer Argast.

Born in Worcester, Mass., Irene was brought to Vermont and the town of South Londonderry as a child of four. She has been here since, attending school, marrying and raising three children.

At the time of Stratton's inception, Irene was working in Peru at Johnny Seesaw's, taking care of the books and the general administrative work. As a close friend of Tink Smith, she offered her services to

the new corporation if it ever got off the ground. Ultimately. Irene was invited to come take care of the office.

The first office was in the Day house which now serves as the headquarters of the Stratton Golf Academy. Then they moved down to the Lincoln Maples Inn which later was to become Haig's. She took care of all the correspondence and communication work for the infant corporation, insuring that all ran smoothly. Two weeks before the opening of the mountain, the offices were finally moved to the fourth floor of the new base lodge.

"The first years were wonderful," she said. "There was a very close family relationship between the employees and never a lack of communication. I remember Peter Pappas, who ran the cafeteria, would steam up from Bennington with six of his employees all stuffed in a Volkswagen. It was marvelous."

The mountain grew by leaps and bounds over the next few years. Even in the summer, Irene maintained the busy office as planning and building continued the year 'round.

"There were many wonderful times back then. One of my favorites was the 'Yankee' Tyrolean Evening held at the end of the season. All the Austrians would help us prepare and rehearse the show with Hans Palmer as the MC. Even Frank put on a show one time with Lederhosen and a big fake nose. A couple of cases of beer and the rehearsal was great."

In 1969, Irene left the mountain to pursue other interests. Two years later she was back on the mountain at the request of Ann Henrich.

"Ann asked if I would come to work for her at the Birkenhaus part time. It seems all my jobs start out as part time and end up being full time," she said with a smile.

She has been an important part of the Birkenhaus ever since, again keeping things in order.

Irene has a tremendous capacity for work and has been an important figure on the mountain for a long time. The corporation owes her and gives her a vote of thanks for all those thankless tasks she has performed.

Harvey Clifford

In 1968, the Stratton Corporation took a major step in its move to prominence in the ski industry by restructuring the management and bringing in a man truly well known and respected in the industry. Previously, the President and General Manager had been separate entities and the management style was not really built on a structured basis. Frank Snyder moved to change this by visiting neighboring Mt. Snow ski area and returning with Harvey Clifford.

Harvey became Stratton's first President and General Manager with the duties of operating and building Stratton according to the plan set forth by its founders.

Of Canadian heritage, Harvey Clifford's life had been devoted to skiing. He developed his skill as a boy on the hill behind his home with a pair of skis purchased at a fire sale for fifty cents. In 1948 he became a member of the Canadian Olympic Team which participated in the games in St. Moritz. Although he didn't win a medal, he was the second best from the North

American continent. After the Olympics, Harvey turned professional to become a coach and a teacher. In 1949 he directed the ski school in Banff, Canada, and then became the coach of the Canadian National Team which he took to the 1952 Olympic games in Oslo, Norway. From 1952 until 1958 he directed ski schools in all corners of the world from New Zealand to Canada and finally ended up at Mt. Snow.

Mt. Snow was a big stepping stone for Harvey. It was here that he stepped into his first administrative work in the ski industry. By the time Frank Snyder came to visit, Harvey was Vice President and General Manager of the Mt. Snow Corporation.

"Frank came to my house one evening and laid out a large plan on the floor of my living room. We discussed it and I made my decision to move to Stratton."

At that time, Mt. Snow was the largest ski area in Southern Vermont. Stratton came along with a different idea of how to market a ski area. The ideas intrigued Harvey and he accepted the challenge.

"Stratton's concept was to appeal to the more social minded skier. They succeeded fairly well. Everything here when I arrived was either first class or aimed in that direction. Still and all there were great challenges. To achieve a first class operation is not an easy task."

Harvey's first challenge came in the form of Vermont's famous Act 250 land use legislation.

"The first thing I heard was what was I going to do about the sewage plant. At that time we were within the law. Then the Act 250 legislation put us out of bounds as far as our waste disposal plant was concerned. It was two years, and a financial struggle, before we finally reached the necessary goal. Back then, anyone could come off the street and speak out against us whether they had a vested interest or not. As a result, the hearings went on forever and ever. Major corporations such as Stratton seemed to be a major target, simply because we had lots of money, or so they believed. Now the process has been defined and only those people involved or with a legitimate claim can speak up at these meetings. All in all I believe it is a very good piece of legislation."

Many more challenges faced Harvey including the continuing negotiations with International Paper. Throughout his entire tenure as President of the Corporation, he worked to insure that Stratton maintained control over its own destiny. The deal was finally worked out after Harvey left when land was donated to the U.S. Ski Educational Foundation.

Under Harvey the mountain began to function more as a business and began to grow and expand into the summer months. The Arnold Palmer Golf Academy, later to become the Stratton Golf Academy, was founded. The Stratton Mountain School came into being, and the first issue of the *Stratton Mountain News* was published. Stratton began to be a true community.

Harvey Clifford had been labeled by some as a fiscal conservative. It was and is his belief that expansion should be limited to the financial capabilities of the area. The result being that the Clifford years were years of growth but also years of financial stability.

"I felt that we should build according to what we could afford. I've seen many places in the industry that have brought problems on themselves by over expansion. People seem to think that real estate sales are the answer and maybe they are to a point, but selling a condominium at a loss is no answer."

He may have been a fiscal conservative, but that didn't stop him from being an innovator. In the years of exceptionally good snow, Stratton limited ticket sales on certain days to keep the liftlines at a minimum.

"I feel that the good PR from the satisfied customer far outweighed anybody who was turned away those few times when it went into effect."

In 1975 Harvey left Stratton and bought the financially troubled Glen Ellen. Soon after, the Sugarbush Corporation bought him out and he retired to Florida with his wife, former Norwegian Olympic skier, Ellen Vera Kaarsburg.

Stratton came a long way under Harvey's guidance. It came from a loosely defined, young member of the industry to a thriving mature part of skiing in the East. It made its first inroads into summer activities as a step toward the ultimate goal of being a year'round resort. One of the major reasons for Stratton's success was the influence of Harvey Clifford.

A. Luke Crispe, Esq.

If you never had the chance to meet Luke Crispe you have missed an experience. He is a self-styled country lawyer (and don't let the "country" part mislead you) with an exceptional legal mind. He is a thoughtful listener, with an impressive ability to analyze whatever the problem or the situation.

After graduating from Indiana Law School in 1933, he was admit-

ted to both the Vermont Bar and the New Hampshire Bar in 1934. He became President of the Vermont Bar Association in 1960–61, and a candidate for Congress in 1958 and a candidate for Governor in 1960, losing the nomination in the Republican Primaries by less than 3000 votes each time. He is a Fellow of the American College of Trial Lawyers. All of this has added up to his being a well-known and colorful figure throughout the state.

Conversations with Luke are a treat, you just sit back, listen and enjoy. With his deep voice and acute observations on almost any subject, he can hold your undivided attention for a long time.

He became one of the five original founding directors of Stratton Corporation in 1960. He served as legal counsel and board member for fourteen years, resigning in 1974. His son, Lawrin, has ably succeeded him as Clerk of the Corporation.

It was Stratton Corporation's good luck to have Luke's wisdom and counseling from the start. The years under his legal guidance were the best years for this fledgling organization, and everyone on the Board was sorry to see him retire. Fortunately, he still has an intense interest in what is happening and keeps in touch. For a man like Luke, who was so much a part of Stratton's beginnings, he will always be concerned about its future.

Luke's interest and activities have been varied. He has served on the Board of Trustees of Grace Cottage Hospital for nearly 30 years. At one time he was involved in the Vermont Chapter of Multiple Sclerosis and served on the original board. He is a former Director of the Ludlow Savings Bank, and also helped with the establishment of the Mt. Ascutney Ski Area.

Emo and Ann Henrich

Stratton has built a huge reputation in the ski industry over the past twenty years. A major reason for this reputation of quality is the presence of Emo Henrich. The talented and dedicated head of the Stratton Ski School, Emo has been with the Stratton Corporation since its inception and has built one of the best ski schools in the country.

A native of Innsbruck, Austria, Emo came to this country in 1955, and has worked to make the not always easy sport of skiing enjoyable to those who wish to learn.

It was in 1960 that Emo and his lovely wife Ann came to Stratton. From the start, Emo could see that the mountain was perfect for a large ski school. The upper and lower areas offered perfect terrain for both beginning and advanced skiers to learn. From a tiny start with only seven instructors, Emo has brought the school forward to one of the largest and most comprehensive in the nation. At present the school offers 22 programs for all levels of skiers from age three on up and employs 65 full-time, 40 part-time and 30 on-call instructors.

It is Emo's talent as an artist, musician and instructor which has given Stratton much of its authentic Austrian flavor. It is Ann's talent as a hostess and her attention to detail which have given the Birkenhaus its true Austrian flavor as well as its impeccable reputation for service and food. Adding to the Austrian atmosphere are the art-

works and carvings that are Emo's work—his devotion to his heritage shows.

But Emo is also a pretty tough guy and a man of action, especially when it comes to helping. In 1956, when he was a ski instructor and mountain guide at Mount Hood, Oregon, 19 young mountain climbers fell into a crevasse and remained helpless for many hours. They were badly injured. Emo was first at the scene and rescued four of the victims by himself; and when additional help arrived he supervised the rescue of the remaining victims.

Ann and Emo are truly the essence of Stratton and they have devoted themselves for the past twenty years to helping make it a special place. Someone once said that "Emo Henrich manages the Stratton Ski School in his own particular way, with guitar and music and Tyrolean charm." Coupled with the energy of his vivacious wife it is a combination that has been very good for Stratton.

Winthrop Hoyt

A long time Bromley Skier, Win Hoyt became affiliated with Stratton during the early planning stages and is one of the original stockholders.

On the day the No. 1 chairlift

made its historic first run up the Suntanner slope Win was aboard, riding behind Frank Snyder and Senator Janeway.

At that time Win was actively engaged in the advertising business in New York City as Chairman of the Charles W. Hoyt advertising agency, and in 1962 the agency was officially appointed to handle all the advertising and public relations for Stratton. The budget for the year was around $20,000, a mere bagatelle by today's standards but, if money was scarce, there was no lack of enthusiasm and ideas.

Win recalls that the main office consisted of one large room shared by the president, the general manager and his assistant. The door was wide open, visitors were always welcome and nobody stood on ceremony. Sometime as many as eight to twelve people would be conferring at the same time but somehow ordered prevailed, everyone pitched in wherever they were needed and a good job was done by all.

Even Lyn Hoyt, Win's wife, was pressed into service at the outset. Lyn had had a successful career in advertising before she married Win and one day, finding Frank at his desk struggling to write copy for the first Stratton brochure while juggling visitors, phone calls, etc. at the same time, Lyn sympathetically offered to take over the writing job.

From then on it was taken for granted that she would do all the copy writing and though the job was not one she sought, it did give her an insight into the continual pursuit of excellence that motivated everyone connected with the development of the mountain. Frank's official edict was that Stratton was going to be the Cadillac of ski areas and no lapse of standards was likely to be missed by his demanding eye.

In 1970 the *Stratton Skier* was launched by Frank and Win as a small newsy periodical reporting on developments and personalities on the mountain. Written, edited and distributed by Win, Frank, Lyn and anyone else who had something to contribute, it grew into the current *Stratton Magazine* with its own editorial staff and an impressive circulation.

Over the years Win worked from his New York office promoting Stratton, spending week-ends at Stratton on business and, of course, skiing.

By the time he retired in 1970 to live in Vermont all year round, the job of directing the growing corporation's advertising and publicity required a full time professional staff, but Win was far too interested to sever all connection with the work and has continued to volunteer his services right up to the present, in any useful capacity.

One job he takes great pleasure in is contacting innkeepers at over a hundred locations in the surrounding area who provide food and lodging for Stratton/Bromley skiers. He keeps them supplied with promotional material for the two ski areas, answers questions and reports on what is happening on the mountain.

Win instituted the annual Innkeepers Party in the base lodge, a popular event at which Stratton plays host to the people whose goodwill is essential. The innkeepers have a chance to meet and talk with key Stratton people and to see for themselves what the area has to offer skiers.

At the age of 80, Win is still an active skier and, at Harvey Clifford's request, he founded the Stratton Senior Skiers Club in 1968. From a small beginning the club has grown steadily and today the membership includes 400 skiers aged 65 and over, and 80 who are over 75 years old. Once a year the members get together for a series of races followed by a convivial cocktail party at the Stratton Mountain Inn, organized by Win and hosted by Stratton to salute a group who prove that skiing can be enjoyed by all ages.

Through his long association with Bromley and Stratton from the pioneer days of both areas, Win is well known to most people in the community and has been dubbed Stratton's "ambassador extraordinaire." He certainly has done as much as anyone to promote skiing in general, Stratton in particular, and he expects to go on enjoying this role for many years to come.

Senator and Mrs. Edward Janeway

In 1945 the town of South Londonderry and the state of Vermont, were fortunate to have been chosen by Mr. Edward Janeway and his wife, the former Elinor White of New York, as their place of residence.

To list the accomplishments of Senator and Mrs. Janeway would take up a tremendous amount of space. Suffice it to say that they have both given of themselves to the state of Vermont in many ways. Both have been appointed to numerous positions of importance, promoting the state culturally and politically. The Senator has been a member of the Vermont House of Representatives and the Vermont Senate as well as a town leader, farmer and businessman. Mrs. Janeway has been involved with the cultural aspect of the state, having served on Governor appointed positions supporting the arts.

In 1959, the founders of Stratton were in need of two very important things. They needed the support of local people and they needed an introduction to the government of Vermont. One of the first and most important decisions made by the young corporation was to seek the help and advice of Senator Edward Janeway. An important area figure, not only did he hold an important and influential position in the state, but more important to the fledgling corporation, he held the respect and admiration of the all important local citizenry.

At the outset, Senator Janeway was appointed as a director of the corporation. He worked diligently with the others in efforts to raise money for the new venture. As did the others, he laid himself on the line both financially and personally to insure the success of Stratton.

In those early days as in the early days of any new development, there was a mistrust and apprehension at what was happening at Stratton. These were the days of outrage at uncontrolled development prior to the passage of Act 250 legislation. The support and presence of Senator Janeway combined with the commitment of the corporation to achieve the highest standard of development, took Stratton through these initial days into the prominent position it holds today.

Elinor Janeway at this time was heavily involved with the arts on a state wide level having been appointed to a commission on the arts by the governor. It was she who came up with the idea for the Stratton Arts Festival and founded it with Kay Smith. From a three day event in its first year, the festival has grown to become the largest short term festival of the arts in the state, exhibiting the works and performances of over 300 of Vermont's best known artists.

Senator and Mrs. Janeway are leaders. They are quiet leaders with engaging smiles whose graciousness and quiet charm are all too unfamiliar today. He is the epitome of the gentleman farmer, the country squire whom everyone looks to for guidance, she a cultured and gracious lady. These descriptions may seem hyperbolic, but are nonetheless true.

Over the years the mountain has changed a great deal from that first family style resort. It has taken on new attitudes that perhaps the good senator does not agree with. Yet still he stands behind the mountain. His presence and influence are felt no matter what decisions are made. Both he and his wife have placed an indelible mark on this development that shall never be removed.

Arthur E. "Tex" Laidlaw

Tex Laidlaw was a bus driver for the Arnold Palmer Golf Academy when it opened in 1971. Today, he is Vice President of Operations.

Laidlaw spent four seasons on Casey Rowley's Ski Patrol before becoming part of Rowley's golf course fairway crew in the summer of 1971. From there he switched to driving the Golf Academy bus, which shuttled youngsters between the training site, golf course, and their rooms.

But Tex was more than a bus driver, especially to the youngsters. He worked with the young golfers, spent time with them if they became ill, and applied first aid skills acquired as a ski patrolman whenever one of the youngsters needed minor medical attention for a scrape or bruise.

When the Academy concluded its first season, Tex returned to the golf course, this time to work in the pro shop with country club professional Elmer Reed.

When the pro shop closed, Ralph Rawson asked Tex to help coordinate construction on the Carlos Otis Clinic.

By Christmas, Harvey Clifford, who was then president and general manager of the Stratton Corporation, made Tex a trouble shooter for the vice presidents. Since that time, the Cooperstown, New York native has made snow, worked with the lift crews, worked on summer maintenance, worked with Vice President Gary Plante on ticket control and sales, and much more—actually pitching in wherever he is needed.

His responsibilities cover a lot of territory, making sure that the day to day operations of all departments are running smoothly.

Tex, a graduate of St. Paul's Preparatory and Syracuse University, is still certified by the Professional Ski Patrol of America and occasionally rejoins Casey's team of patrolmen when he's needed; something which he thoroughly enjoys.

"Stratton Pioneers" gather at Birkenhaus to commemorate long-standing service to the Company: (from left, back row) Allen Hodge, Dick Smith, Gary West, Karl Dietrich, Pat Williams, Donald Greene, Casey Rowley, Emo Henrich, Karl Bauer and Don Roberts; (center row) Win Hoyt, Senator Ed Janeway, Hans Palmer, Lester Williams, Tink Smith and Ralph Rawson; (front row) Edith Davison, Betty Gotshall, Ruth Rowley, Lee Landman and Irene Benson.

Bud Lench

Stratton Mountain is a special ski area in many ways. One of the most obvious to the first timer who has been to other areas, is the complete lack of commercialism, neon and clutter, specifically along the access road. A drive along any other ski area access road is a sideshow of fast food and souvenirs. Not so with Stratton. Esthetically it is one of the most beautiful resorts to be found anywhere.

The result of this careful planning is that the clientele who have invested their time and money here are part of the Stratton community which pays particular attention to the design and care of the area. The man responsible for at least 50 of the homes of these people in design and concept is Charles "Bud" Lench an architect and designer out of the Boston area. He is not only responsible for many of the homes, including founder Frank Snyder's, but he is also responsible for the design and function of the interior of the base lodge.

Bud's involvement came as the result of his design work for Peter Pappas, Stratton's first food and beverage manager. Bud was designing a restaurant for Pappas when Peter asked him to come and look at the kitchen design in the Stratton Base Lodge. Pappas had fears that the original design was going to cause problems as far as functional flow. Bud agreed and came up to see what he could do. Six months later, the corporation founders asked him to design and finish the base lodge and its furnishings, right down to the eagles on the chandeliers.

Bud moved to Stratton and stayed in a house owned by Pearl Buck, who owned a great deal of property in the area.

"I was driving down Taylor Hill Road one day and passed a lady walking. I stopped and asked her if she would like a lift. She asked me immediately what I was doing in the area and I told her that I was working on the mountain. I also told her that I was looking for a place to live. She then directed me to one of her three houses, this one being known as Forest Haunt, and told me I could live there. Simple as that. She was quite a remarkable lady."

Bud stayed on the mountain and became more and more involved with the construction. His design included the Norse House under the direction of Charles Sonnenfeld and Peter Pringham. Many of his designs have yet to be built including the Eagle's Nest on top of the mountain.

One of Bud's first indirect contributions to the area was his purchase of a barn on the Winhall Hollow Road. This became known as Bud's Bunks and at that time was one of the only places in the area with available lodging.

"This place was a virtual wilderness. Outside of Johnny Seesaw's, there was no lodging outside of Manchester. The access road was a horror show back then but really quite funny. We had to haul people up the mountain with tractors, garbage trucks, four wheel drive vehicles or anything else that could make it. During the Spring thaw it was a quagmire. Right in front of the 16th hole of the golf course is a yellow Volkswagen that sank, and it is still there to this day. The people jumped out as it sank and hopped on a truck going by."

Bud is responsible for a great deal of Stratton's esthetic value. Many people have put their trust in his talent and have been rewarded with the beautiful homes that dot the mountainside today. Bud is a controversial and outspoken gentleman who at times disagrees with Stratton and its policies. Nevertheless, his work speaks for itself as an integral part of what Stratton is today.

Minor E. (Mitch) McLaughlin

Mitch McLaughlin came to Stratton when the offices were still located in the "Maples." Mitch had been at Mt. Snow for seven years (since its inception) and had first hand knowledge of a ski area's "growing pains." In addition to his PR duties at Mt. Snow, he acquired a general knowledge of what makes a ski area tick, and it was this knowledge that was to be of great benefit to Stratton as it rolled towards opening its doors.

He became Stratton's first Public Relations Director, and later became Assistant Manager. He was a fountain of knowledge and promotional ideas, such as the "Name the Trails contest" (which provided the first mailing list); he had excellent PR relationships with all the media on the East Coast and had many friends among the skiing greats of that time. But he also knew how to train lift operators, instruct personnel, and keep customers happy. Always with a genial and pleasant manner.

In 1968, deciding the time had come to start his own business, he resigned from Stratton. Mitch is now established in his own consulting firm in League City, Texas, many miles away from the mountain he so ably helped promote.

Carlos G. Otis

In the very late thirties, a very animated and dedicated man walked into Townshend, Vermont and began a career which was to affect virtually every man, woman and child in the rural West River Valley.

Dr. Carlos Otis is a driven man, driven to serve and dedicated to the care of all those who walk through his doors. It makes no difference about ability to pay. If the care is needed, it is given.

Through those early years he worked incessantly, making his rounds from home to home of the people in need of his care, stopping only to eat at the home of the person he happened to be with at the time.

"Back then I knew everyone in the valley. I knew how many cows they had, how much milk they produced and how much maple syrup they put up. Many times I was paid with a bushel of corn or a half a hog. I really didn't need an office."

During the war, Dr. Otis attempted many times to join the service to do his part. Due to a small medical problem he was rejected. Again and again he tried to enlist with the argument that as a doctor he would have no problems. Unknown to him, the people of the valley had circulated a petition which ultimately came back with 2000 names on it. The petition was to keep him at home, for he was the only doctor in the valley.

"Those days were hectic. I delivered close to 150 babies a year and ran back and forth up and down this valley many times a day."

As the years went by, Dr. Otis decided that there was a need for a hospital in the Townshend area. In 1949 he founded the Grace Cottage Hospital in a house given by Mary L. Plumb, a Townshend teacher, and has been the administrator of it ever since.

Stratton Mountain came into the picture in the early sixties. The founders of the ski area immediately recognized the need for a medical service to take care of the clientele of the mountain. They immediately went to Carlos Otis. A first aid room was set up where the present Real Estate office now is and was staffed by a nurse named Ellen Hart.

"She was a real corker. One of the best nurses I've ever known. She would analyze the injury and then if need be would send them down to me. During those first ten years, we took care of around 5000 fractures. Due to the changes in equipment and the advances in design, the incidence of injury has steadily declined."

In 1970, Phillip Snyder, brother of Frank Snyder, came up with the unique idea of a clinic right on the mountain. No other ski area had such a service and it would be another plus for Stratton's drive toward quality and excellence in service. The Corporation donated the land and the money was funded privately by donation. Because of his service the clinic was named the Carlos Otis Clinic.

Many people thought that perhaps Dr. Otis would move to the mountain and take over the duties as doctor and administrator for the clinic.

"The people in this valley had taken care of me for some 20 plus years and I wasn't about to walk out on them. As a result I set up a rotating service where doctors from the Boston area serviced the clinic in return for lodging and skiing for their families. It has worked very well."

The clinic is now staffed by two Registered Nurses and a full time doctor. Orthopedic doctors come in on a rotating basis during the ski season. Injured skiers are brought in by Stratton's excellent ski patrol and critiqued on the upper floor. If the injury warrants further care, they are moved to the bottom floor for X-ray and if needed, casting. They are then sent home with a copy of the X-ray and instructions to go immediately to their own doctor. The bottom line to all this is that Stratton skiers are under an umbrella of excellent medical care.

Dr. Otis is still the administrator of the clinic and makes all the financial decisions. He is still active in his practice and remains the symbol of comfort to the people in the valley. To date he has delivered 4,598 babies and the number increases steadily.

"I'm shooting for 5,000."

Dr. Otis is a special man. The number of people in the world that do as much service and good to their fellow man are few and far between.

Hans Palmer

For these past twenty years, the "voice of the Stratton Ski School" has been a remarkable man named Hans Palmer.

A native of Gaiz, Austria, Hans has spent the greater part of his life in the United States and served her admirably in World War II.

Hans was educated in England at Cambridge University. He then returned to Austria to gain his Ph.D. in Geography. It was during this period of time that Hitler was moving into Austria, forcing its annexation by armed plebescite. Hans wanted no part of this and moved immediately to Turkey where he taught at an American school. While in Turkey, Hans was named as the coach of Turkish Ski Team for the 1940 Olympics. They were never to be.

At the outbreak of the war, Hans moved to the United States and enlisted in the 43rd Infantry Division as a private. By the war's end, he held the rank of captain and was awarded the Silver Star, Bronze Star, Purple Heart with Oak Leaf Cluster, two Presidential Unit Citations, two meritorious commendation ribbons and had served in both the Pacific and European theaters of the war.

In the early fifties, Hans moved up to Vermont and became the assistant ski school director at Bromley. In 1961 Emo Henrich hired him away to become the assistant at the new Stratton Ski School. Together, Hans and Emo wrote the first manual for the Stratton Ski School. It was Hans who handled the tape recorder for the first Tyrolean Evenings before the formation of the Stratton Mountain Boys.

The school grew over the years, becoming larger and more involved as things do. As more and more people began to come, Hans moved to the ski school desk and the administration of that all important staging area. At this time the ski school desk was at the top of the main stairs on the main floor of the base lodge. Here Hans handled the ski school as well as information and ticket sales. Soon Hans' voice became a fixture over the intercom and he became the official spokesman for Stratton and the Stratton Ski School.

Since the beginning, Hans has directed literally thousands of skiers to the right place at the right time. His smiling face and quiet demeanor have been the trademarks of the ski school desk and he has been the heart of the operation since its inception.

Hans retired from Stratton in the Spring of 1981. Men of his caliber are few and far between and Stratton will be hard pressed to replace him. To those who have grown up on the mountain, the familiar "Velcom to Strrratton Mountain" will be sorely missed.

Ralph Rawson

Edward Rawson, an ancestor of Ralph's, was secretary of the Massachusetts Colony for 32 years, and was charged with the responsibility of dispersing the land and reporting periodically to the king. Of course, this was often a difficult task, considering the rebellious nature of many of the colonists.

But Edward Rawson was a shrewd man. He carved crude boundaries into the land with the aplomb of a politician, and reported the best of news to the king. Later he chose to withdraw his allegiance to the throne, thousands of leagues away, and invest it in new found freedom and the future of the young colonies. He was rewarded by the colonial frontiersmen who named a hamlet (in what would one day be known as Southern Vermont) in his honor—Rawsonville.

Today we have Ralph Rawson, who in the tradition of his heritage, is a vice president of the Stratton Corporation and charged with considerable responsibility.

Ralph Rawson was down a manhole, trying to unplug it, when a voice from above shouted to him that he had just been named a vice president of the Stratton Corporation. That was in 1967.

Back then, he had a nook in the rear of the lowest level of the base lodge, and there he spread out the maps of his trade. Suddenly, he was whisked upstairs.

It took a while for Ralph to get used to his management role, not that the idea of being an executive was not appealing. But Ralph was—and still is—the kind of person who needs to see the fruit of his labor.

"I was never comfortable doing work that couldn't be measured. You can measure the work of real estate sales or the Food and Beverage Department," he explained, "but how do you measure someone like me? All my life I've been an overhead item."

Thus, it has been the creative planning and designing aspect of his work which has given him the most pleasure. And, once executed, there is a yardstick by which he can be measured.

After his eighteenth birthday, Ralph joined the marines. When he got out he came back to Vermont to work on the stretch of road from Bondville to the West. Before long, he had his own survey party and was reassigned to work on the super highway system which links the New England states.

Four years and nine months later, Rawson completed his work on Interstate 91 from the Massachusetts line up to Bellows Falls and took a job with a small engineering firm in Brattleboro.

With the Brattleboro firm he learned the art of developing profiles for chairlift systems. But, after about a year, the Federal government's flood control project in Townshend, Vermont was begun. It was 1958 and Ralph Rawson became a transitman.

But the job was over in two years. The company would send him to Niagara, New York or Hartford, Connecticut he knew. But he now had three children and did not want to leave the area. On a Sunday in November 1960, Ralph drove up to the construction-site of a new ski area.

There, Rawson met Elmer Argast, who was in charge of operations, and a few days later was called back. That was December 1, 1960, and he became liaison between the planning and construction units on the mountain. He was one of four men who worked through the winter.

There still was no access road to the Mountain from Bondville when Ralph laid out the first streets.

During those early years the work crews put in 60 hours a week, and sometimes more.

"It would be hard to get that number of men to do all that variety of work today."

In a matter of months, Rawson began the coordination and layout of Stratton's 18-hole golf course. With compass and tape in hand, he scaled several of the holes himself, improvising from landmark to landmark.

When Harvey Clifford took over duties as president and general manager of the corporation, his reshaping of management called for

Karl Dietrich and his companion, Duke: multilingual night watchman from the beginning and a helpful friend to many Stratton skiers.

the creation of a personnel department. The mountain then employed approximately 340 people in the winter, a staff of 100 people in the summer, and Ralph Rawson was appointed head of that department.

Today, Ralph Rawson is Vice President of Construction and Maintenance, a complex and important responsibility which he handles exceedingly well.

"Give anyone a minute or two of your time. You don't have to agree, but the other person will feel better," said Ralph, recalling a maxim he has adopted during his years at Stratton.

David A. Rosow

A new chapter began in the 90 odd year history of Stratton's parent company, Moore & Munger, Inc., when David Rosow took over from Frank Snyder as President and Chief Executive Officer in October, 1981.

An enthusiastic skier and golfer, David brings youth and vigor to the Stratton scene. A 1964 graduate of the University of Minnesota, David served in the U.S. Navy for three years during the Viet Nam War, ending up as a qualified Officer of The Deck aboard the U.S.S. Forrestal, one of our larger aircraft carriers.

In 1974, David joined Moore & Munger as Snyder's assistant after several years in the Wall Street investment banking business, and it was not long before he became President of two of Moore & Munger's operating subsidiaries, the Cross Oil Development Company and Cross Development Company, before being advanced to the top position in the Company.

With his lovely wife Jean and two sons, David, Jr. and Christopher, David now has Stratton as his second home. He is dedicated to carrying on the Stratton Corporation's commitment to quality.

Casey Rowley

Casey came to Stratton Mountain to organize and direct a ski patrol in the spring of 1960. But before snow was on the ground and the mountain readied for its first skiers, Casey was a part of the crew that cut trails, chased the ever present porcupines out of the construction areas and lent a capable hand wherever he was needed. He was also at the summit, on that memorable day for Stratton when a high powered helicopter air-lifted and set the towers for the ski lifts, helping to guide the pilot and his assistant over the dropoff site.

Starting with only a handful of men—5 to be exact—Casey went on to organize and head the Stratton Ski Patrol, which is today recognized as one of the best in the nation. The patrol itself is to a large extent a volunteer organization and is made up of about 154 members who work mainly on busy weekends and holiday weeks. These volunteers work together with Stratton's own full and part-time paid patrollers.

Casey Rowley, who is a native Vermonter and a beloved one, headed Stratton's Ski Patrol since the day it opened. Not only is he a certified National Patroller, he is also a member and founder of the Professional Ski Patrol, with many life saving awards to his credit.

Today Casey has a new position—Mountain Manager—and after 21 years on Stratton working in various capacities with numerous titles, there is probably no one better qualified to handle this big job.

Casey Rowley's Recollections

When we asked Casey to tell us something about his childhood days and his learning to ski here in Vermont, he obliged with the following:

"When I first started skiing it was on skis bought at the local hardware store. Everyone bought their skis at the hardware store in those days, except perhaps those who ordered them from the Montgomery Ward catalogue. Anyway, they more or less all looked alike. Kinda wide, with varnished wood and wide leather straps across the middle where you shoved in your feet. Like skiing in a pair of slippers. Most everyone skied in their rubber galoshes—you know the sort of high rubber boots with the buckles for closing—or if you were lucky you had sturdy, waterproof shoes called "Hi-Cuts." You weren't anybody unless you had a pair of those particular shoes.

Anyway, we kids all had a problem learning to ski because there wasn't a way to hold the feet firmly on the skis as you went down the hill. Most of the time it was pure luck that the skis were still on your feet when you got to the bottom. It wasn't long before some kid discovered that those heavy canning jar rubbers (swiped from your Mom's canning supplies) if wrapped around the heel of your galoshes and secured to something up front helped keep the skis on. It was some improvement, but my brother and I had a better invention—we just hammered a nail through our new "Hi-Cuts" right into the skis! Of course, we had a big problem with our parents when they finally found out what we had done.

Somehow we learned to ski and loved it. In spite of no poles, no edges on the skis, and the only direction to go was straight down with no turns. It was rare if any of us kids hurt ourselves, except those few times when we hit a tree or ran into a stonewall. Boy, were those skis hard to turn.

Little by little both the skis and my skiing improved, which doesn't mean that I had become anything resembling an expert. But by now I had taken to skiing at Bromley which was a real big deal for me. One day as I was zooming down a slope—I thought I was doing it in great style—I crashed and broke my skis right in front of Bromley's first Ski School Director, Otto Lang, who was instructing a class. Oh, was I mad, and embarrassed. But the man was a real gentleman, and I'll never forget him. He took the time to go and find a pair of skis for me. He gave them to me, and even though they weren't new and they showed a bit of wear, those skis were pretty special. He had made one young fellow pretty happy. From then on I had the skiing bug, and it was right there at Bromley a few years later that I became involved in their very first ski patrol program."

Frank V. Snyder
Chairman of the Board
The Stratton Corporation

When someone asked Frank's wife, Jessie, if she could describe her husband in 200 words or less, she quickly answered, "It is impossible to reduce Frank to 200 pounds or 200 words!" The truth about this statement at least about the 200 words, became apparent as the list of accomplishments and interests were gathered and put together for this profile. Untold numbers of words could be written about Frank V. Snyder—the nature of the man and his many talents. His human shortcomings, and his always dominant role in whatever he is involved in—either business or pleasure—and the tempo at which he moves which can only be described as going full blast.

Frank has long been a physical fitness buff and the great outdoors is his natural element. He excels at sports, especially skiing and his skill at sailing is legendary. He has a deep appreciation for good music, has a fine voice, which he loves to raise in song, and takes pleasure in playing the piano and organ. Influenced by his good friend, Emo Henrich, painting has become another of his serious hobbies and another definite talent. He is a published writer ("Life Under Sail" published by MacMillan in 1963), and a man of vision whose aims are high, but rarely exceed his grasp. It is in fact very probable that without him Stratton would never have come into being. A successful businessman, he has strong convictions and makes swift decisions. When Frank chairs a meeting there is no doubt who is in charge. He may appear to ride rough-shod over the opposition at times, but he is far from inflexible and will look at both sides of the question if presented with cogent reasons. He is a big man in more ways than one, and if he feels he has been in error he is quick to say "I am sorry"—and there is no doubting the sincerity of his words.

Frank was born in Bayside, Long Island, New York in 1922 and received his education at the Taft School, Harvard College, and University of Virginia Law School. He married the former Jessie Pennoyer and they have four children and one grandchild. From 1948 to 1950 he was an associate at the law firm of Root, Ballantine, Harlan, Bushby and Palmer. He was the former president and is now Chairman of the Board of Moore & Munger, Inc. and is responsible for bringing the company to a position of one of the world's largest independent producers and marketers of lubricating oils and waxes. He served with the U.S. Navy from 1943 to 1946 and saw submarine duty in both the Atlantic and Pacific. Other activities include: President of the National Ski Areas Association, 1971–1973 and a Trustee of the Mystic Seaport Museum and the New York Yacht Club.

Donald Tarinelli

Back in 1975 when the Corporation was searching for a Vice President and General Manager of Ski Operations they happily found a man suited for the job right in their own back yard.

That man was Don Tarinelli, who had recently retired from his family business in Connecticut and was looking for a new challenge. Don had spent a lot of time with his family on Stratton Mountain, having been a chalet owner since 1963, and was a familiar figure in this mountain community. He had become involved in the Junior Racing Program due to the active participation of his four children, all of whom were avid skiers, and subsequently became a prime mover in this important program.

But perhaps more significant in the choice of Tarinelli for the position was his background, which was excellent. With a degree in Civil Engineering from Massachusetts Institute of Technology, and graduate work at Columbia University in land planning and architecture, along with business experience in his father's construction firm, Tarinelli was a natural.

In August 1975, he permanently moved to Stratton with his wife, Vivian, and assumed the duties which eventually led to his becoming President of the Corporation.

Tarinelli accomplished a great many things while he was in charge and he is justifiably proud of them—the expansion of Stratton into a year round recreational resort with the beginning of the John Newcombe Tennis Center, The Golf Academy at Stratton, and the purchase and expansion of the

Stratton Mountain Inn. Making a truly impressive summer recreation complex on top of an impressive mountain.

He was also responsible for the beginning of a successful real estate development with the construction and sales of the Shattarack and Styles Brook Condominiums. All this along with the expansion of the Base Lodge complex and other major construction projects. Don's love and knowledge of the building business is evident in all his accomplishments. But he deserves special credit for bringing to a satisfactory conclusion the interminable negotiations with International Paper. A major achievement.

Don's enthusiasm for the future of Stratton Mountain is catching. Just listen to him for a few minutes and, if you weren't one already, you become a Stratton booster. He makes you a believer, and you can't help but admire both his optimism and the progress his efforts have made in this successful resort community.

Elmer Argast

Elmer came to South Londonderry, Vermont, by way of Newark, New Jersey, where he was born and raised. He attended the local schools and went on to Rutgers University for a few semesters. But, this was depression time and when the opportunity came to work for Reynolds Metals, Elmer didn't hesitate—he took the job. When World War II came along Elmer spent five long years with the New Jersey National Guard as Advanced Infantry Training Instructor. Then it was back to Reynolds Metals, as General Foreman of their Harrison, New Jersey plant.

In 1950 he moved to Vermont, and when asked what prompted the move, his answer was, "Because I liked it." Elmer also had been watching the changes taking place in New Jersey and felt they weren't for the better. One day he decided to count the traffic lights he had to go through on his way to work. There were 65 of them! On top of that, the time consumed in just getting to the Reynolds' plant was nearly an hour each way. That was it! For Elmer the time had come to leave. The year was 1950 and he moved bag and baggage to South Londonderry, where he purchased a small grocery store and settled into the quiet life of small town Vermont.

But it was not to last forever, because it was inevitable that his background with Reynolds Metals would become known and along with it his capability to direct and coordinate large projects. It appeared to Tink Smith and Frank Snyder that this was just the man they needed, and he soon became one of the hardest working and most valuable members of that beginning Stratton group, holding the position of General Manager for nearly four years.

Lester Williams

Lester was born and raised in Londonderry, Vermont, living the simple and honest life of the north country lumberman. In his life he held only three jobs. He was a lumberman during the majority of his youth. After the mill burned down he went to work as a bulldozer operator on the Ball Mountain Dam. Two years later he was the second man on the Stratton payroll.

When Lester was hired by Stratton there literally was no Stratton. It was virtually all on paper. He began work on the base lodge site the first winter driving his bulldozer with its unheated cab, preparing the way for spring construction. It was Lester and others who cleared the trails and over the year built the golf course. It was the huge blade of Lester's bulldozer that scooped out the three and a half million gallon reservoir.

Lester remembers those days when many times during those cold mornings the machines just wouldn't start. The maintenance building was a small shack with a piece of canvas for a door. It would be difficult today to get skilled operators to work under such inconvenient conditions. But Vermonters like Lester Williams were uncomplaining and went about their work making the best of it.

Lester continued to work through the years for the Stratton Corporation and became their first 10 year employee. For his efforts he was made the head of the maintenance department; and an elaborate maintenance area was constructed with storage rooms, locker rooms and a blueprint room for the engineer. Giant bays for servicing the mountain's considerable amount of heavy equipment, and a huge parts department make up the rest of the maintenance building. Under his supervision all the many types of vehicles from snowcats to the fire trucks were maintained in top notch condition.

In 1981 Lester retired after 20 years of service to the Corporation. In his honor a dinner was given and as a sign of love and respect, the men of maintenance gave him a trip to the islands out of their own pockets, pockets which are many times not that full.

It is this kind of respect and love that Williams deserved for the 20 years of untiring efforts against sometimes intolerable conditions.

Index